Cambridge Elements

Elements in Global Ph
editec
Yujin Nag
University of C

THE AFRICAN *MOOD* PERSPECTIVE ON GOD AND THE PROBLEM OF EVIL

Ada Agada
Federal University Otuoke

CAMBRIDGE
UNIVERSITY PRESS

CAMBRIDGE
UNIVERSITY PRESS

Shaftesbury Road, Cambridge CB2 8EA, United Kingdom

One Liberty Plaza, 20th Floor, New York, NY 10006, USA

477 Williamstown Road, Port Melbourne, VIC 3207, Australia

314–321, 3rd Floor, Plot 3, Splendor Forum, Jasola District Centre, New Delhi – 110025, India

103 Penang Road, #05–06/07, Visioncrest Commercial, Singapore 238467

Cambridge University Press is part of Cambridge University Press & Assessment, a department of the University of Cambridge.

We share the University's mission to contribute to society through the pursuit of education, learning and research at the highest international levels of excellence.

www.cambridge.org
Information on this title: www.cambridge.org/9781009452663

DOI: 10.1017/9781009452694

© Ada Agada 2024

When citing this work, please include a reference to the DOI 10.1017/9781009452694

First published 2024

A catalogue record for this publication is available from the British Library

ISBN 978-1-009-45266-3 Hardback
ISBN 978-1-009-45268-7 Paperback
ISSN 2976-5749 (online)
ISSN 2976-5730 (print)

The African *Mood* Perspective on God and the Problem of Evil

Elements in Global Philosophy of Religion

DOI: 10.1017/9781009452694
First published online: November 2024

Ada Agada
Federal University Otuoke

Author for correspondence: Ada Agada, agadaaa@fuotuoke.edu.ng

Abstract: This Element concisely and critically explores the African limited God perspective that denies that the categories of omnipotence, omniscience, and omnibenevolence are applicable to the God of African Traditional Religion (ATR). The Element teases out the intricate conceptual nuances in the limitation thesis and interrogates the divergent stances of proponents of the limited God view, with special focus on the *mood* perspective of the philosophy of consolationism. Proponents of the limitation thesis may be limited God theists who accept that the limited God is a creator-deity or, at least, a world-designer, or they may be limited God non-theists who deny the limited God personality and agency. The Element expands the frontiers of research in African philosophy of religion by showing that the limitation thesis raises the question of a limited God's moral responsibility for some of the evil in the world in his capacity as a world-creator or world-designer.

Keywords: limited God thesis, African limited God view, African philosophy of religion, consolation God, problem of evil

ISBNs: 9781009452663 (HB), 9781009452687 (PB), 9781009452694 (OC)
ISSNs: 2976-5749 (online), 2976-5730 (print)

Contents

General Introduction

African philosophy of religion is a very young field of African philosophy broadly construed. It has recently established itself as a vibrant field of African philosophy, thanks to the commitment of African philosophers like Jonathan O. Chimakonam, Aribiah D. Attoe, Motsamai Molefe, and Emmanuel Ofuasia, and of Western scholars who work on African philosophy like Thaddeus Metz and Kirk Lougheed, as well as the support of the Yujin Nagasawa–led Global Philosophy of Religion Project that has graciously provided sorely needed financial support. A major development in African philosophy of religion is the eclipsing of traditional African theism by what is now regarded as the African limited God view.

While traditional African theism holds a position that traditional Christian theism fully endorses, with its claim of God possessing the omni-properties, the limited God view asserts that the African conception of God is properly one that presents the deity as limited in power, knowledge, and goodness. A category of African philosophers of religion now go by the label limited God theists. Limited God theists concede that God has great powers but deny that his power, knowledge, and goodness are of the order of omnipotence, omniscience, and omnibenevolence. Limited God theists have reimagined the idea of God and the problem of evil in very novel and interesting ways. This Element takes debates in the limited God school to a new level with its critical and constructive focus.

This Element is structured into three critical sections of varying lengths. Section 1, titled 'African Philosophy of Religion', demonstrates the existence of both a transcendental or perfect God perspective and a limited God view in African Traditional Religion (ATR). The section introduces the reader to the limited God view and provides an adequate context for this increasingly dominant view. The section highlights the way African philosophers present the limited God in the vitalist and non-vitalist traditions. Section 2, titled 'The Limitation Thesis and the Problem of Evil', continues the literature review commenced in Section 1 and introduces the dimension of the problem of evil. The section delineates the powers of the limited God and notes that in much of the literature, the limited God is an entity that possesses considerable power even if this power is not of the order of omnipotence. The section poses a number of questions. Does the concept of limitation imply that the problem of evil in the world does not arise in the context of the limited God view? Does limitation imply absolute incapacity? If God is not the cause of evil, where is the evil in the world coming from? If God is a knowledgeable being who foresees at least some of the evils that will proliferate in the world just before creating the world, why does he go on to express his creative powers? Is there a necessity at work that compels him to create even against his better judgement? Is the limited God morally responsible for the evil in the world despite not being the cause of evil?

In Section 3, titled 'The Limited God, Creation, and Moral Responsibility', I respond to all of these questions from the perspective of consolation philosophy, my own contribution to African philosophy. In this final section, the longest in this Element, I assert that the limited consolation God is a passible being who bears moral responsibility for the evil in the world, a being powerful, knowledgeable, and good who can be deemed to be working to ameliorate the suffering in the world. Section 3 properly presents the consolation God in an exercise that I hope will contribute to global philosophy of religion.

1 African Philosophy of Religion
1.1 Introduction

In this introductory section, I review the limited God literature and identify the non-vitalist and vitalist traditions of the limitation thesis. I use the terms *world* and *universe* frequently in the section. I use them interchangeably to indicate the totality in which all things persist. Where a distinction is made between the two terms, I explain the specific way that the term involved is used. The section is divided into several subsections. Subsection 1.2 contextualises the limited God view in African philosophy of religion and contrasts this view with traditional African theism which presents God as a perfect being. Subsection 1.3 properly introduces the limitation thesis. Subsections 1.4 and 1.5 concisely explore the limited God literature in the non-vitalist and vitalist traditions respectively. Subsection 1.6 introduces the conception of God articulated in the philosophy of consolationism. Subsection 1.7 is the conclusion.

1.2 Two Conceptions of God in African Traditional Religion (ATR) and African Philosophy of Religion

African Traditional Religion (ATR) does not have a written holy book.[1] Its sources include myths, proverbs, wise sayings, and the world views of traditional African societies. African Traditional Religion furnishes two broad conceptions of God that African philosophers of religion have relied on in the

---

[1] The singular form African Traditional Religion was popularised by scholars like Edward Geoffrey Parrinder (1954), E. Bolaji Idowu (1973), and John S. Mbiti (1975). The rationale for the singular 'religion' rather than the plural 'religions' is the remarkable similarity of the religious phenomena and practices of diverse traditional African societies which justify certain generalisations about African religion, notwithstanding the cultural diversity of sub-Saharan African groups (see Shaw 1990; Burley 2020).

construction of theories about God's nature and his relation with the world. In this Element, I will label the two dominant conceptions of God 'traditional African theism' and 'the limited God view'. African Traditional Religion itself is a term widely used in African religious studies literature to refer to the religious belief system of traditional African societies, their worship practices and cosmogonies. It is characterised by belief in the existence of God, deities, ancestors, and cosmic forces and principles that human beings can manipulate for good or ill (see, for example, Parrinder 1954; Mbiti 1969, 1975; Idowu 1973).

Traditional African theism reflects belief in God as the supreme being and personal creator of the world who possesses the superlative properties of omnipotence, omniscience, and omnibenevolence. Early defenders of traditional African theism like Joseph Boakye Danquah (1944), E. Bolaji Idowu (1962), John S. Mbiti (1969), Joseph Omosade Awolalu and P. Adelumo Dopamu (1979), and E. Ikenga-Metuh (1981) argue from a decolonisation perspective that traditional African societies developed autochthonous conceptions of God as the supreme being who possesses the omni-properties. In its early form, the decolonisation project in African religious studies marks a defensive reaction against long-established Western racist prejudices (see, for example, Hume 1987; Njoku 2002; p'Bitek 2011; Agada 2022a). In the nineteenth century, Georg Wilhelm Friedrich Hegel noted that Africans lack not only the capacity for rational thinking but also conscious awareness of the existence of a transcendent supernatural entity – that is, God (see Hegel 2001, 111–113).[2] In Europe, Hegel promoted the view that ATR is not a religion in the sense that Christianity, for example, is a religion with a distinct object of worship that is considered a divine person separate from nature. Early decolonisation scholars set for themselves the goal of demonstrating that Africans have conceptions of God that correspond to the Christian conception of a perfect creator-God.

The early decolonisation scholars asserted that Western scholarship misinterprets and inferiorises ATR. They set out to formulate what they consider the correct African perspective on God. They claimed that traditional African

---

[2] The racist assertion by Western philosophers like Hegel ([1824] 2001) that Africans have an inferior philosophical capacity has spawned the rationality question, one of the long-running debates in African philosophy. African philosophers have generally rejected the racist claim and have asserted that the concept of rationality is a thick concept not amenable to a universal definition. They accuse the West of imposing its own particularist understanding of rationality on the world and labelling this perspective the universal view (for details, see, for example, L. S. Senghor (1964), Cheikh Anta Diop (1974), John O. Sodipo (1975), Peter Bodunrin (1981), Theophilus Okere (1983), C. S. Momoh (1985), Mogobe B. Ramose (1991), Innocent C. Onyewuenyi (1993), D. A. Masolo (1994), V.-Y. Mudimbe (1988), Mabogo P. More (1996), Olufemi Taiwo (1998), Barry Hallen (2002), Lucius Outlaw (2004), M. Akin Makinde (2007), J. Obi Oguejiofor (2009), Fainos Mangena (2014), and Bernard Matolino (2015).

societies hold views of God that are not inferior to the Christian view of God. African philosophers like Maduabuchi Dukor (1990), Kwame Gyekye (1995), and Ebunoluwa O. Oduwole (2007) have endorsed the traditional theistic stance and presented the God of ATR as a perfect being. African theists like Gyekye, Oduwole, and Francis O. C. Njoku (2002) have focused philosophical effort on demonstrating that traditional African societies have autochthonous conceptions of God as a perfect being. There is less interest in the project of proving the existence of God by force of argument (see Lougheed, Molefe, and Metz 2024).

Gyekye reaches the conclusion that the Akan God, Onyame, is omnipotent, omniscient, omnibenevolent, and omnipresent after extensively analysing Akan proverbs, wise sayings, myths, and names and titles of God in the Akan language. Paving the way for the articulation of an African theodicy, Gyekye (1995, 70) affirms that:

> Onyame is the Absolute Reality, the origin of all things, the absolute ground, the sole and whole explanation of the universe, the source of all existence . . . Onyame transcends time and is thus free from the limitation of time, an eternity without beginning, without an end ... While containing space, Onyame is not held to be spatial. He is not bound or limited to any particular region of space. He is omnipresent (_enyiasombea_), all-pervading.

But having arrived at the idea of a perfect being through the analysis of traditional Akan linguistic phenomena and world views, Gyekye (1995, 116) struggles to articulate a convincing theodicy to account for God permitting evil in the world. He suggests that moral evil arises from human misuse of free will while physical evil can be attributed to the influence of malevolent forces active in the world. However, the appeal to free will does not succeed because Gyekye accepts that God fixes a human being's destiny before birth. He attempts a compatibilist balancing act with the claim that while God fixes the individual's destiny, he does not rigidly condition minute details of the individual's life. Destiny affects only key events and basic attributes of the individual. Underlining the Akan belief in theological determinism, Gyekye (1995, 113) quotes the proverb 'God's destiny cannot be altered (_Onyame hyɛbea yennae no_).' But realising that there is a problem reconciling free will and determinism, Gyekye (1995, 115) notes: 'What these basic attributes are is of course difficult to say with certainty. Nevertheless, it is clear that the Akan notion of destiny is a general one, which implies that not everything that a person does or that happens to him or her represents a page from the "book of destiny".'

According to Gyekye, the omnipotent God gives humans unalterable destinies from the beginning. Since he is all-good, the destiny he gives is a good one. He is an omniscient being who foresees future human actions. This perfect

God would have ensured the actualisation of every (good) human destiny to prevent the suffering one finds in the world. Free will does not appear to be a great good that a perfect God must preserve at the cost of allowing evil in the world since he fixes destinies *ab initio*. Given his ability to do every logically possible thing (that is, things not contrary to reason or logic, like creating a world and not creating a world simultaneously), he ought to have suppressed the malevolent activities of malevolent spirits that he created. It can even be asserted that since the omnipotent God created lesser deities and spirits, he should have created evil-causing entities as good beings. Note that Gyekye's God determines the future trajectory of the world from the very beginning. In this deterministic world, God must have given the lesser deities a good destiny at the time he created them, as was the case with humans. A good destiny involves not acting malevolently or perversely. Accordingly, a possible appeal to the free will of the lesser deities to explain God allowing them to choose to act malevolently does not succeed.

As suggested earlier, a free-will defence must fail because Gyekye does not succeed in reconciling theological determinism with free will. Merely saying that some things are determined while others lie outside the sway of determinism does not establish the truth of compatibilism. If determinism is true, then it may be that even the choices that human beings make are conditioned by ethical, social, legal, cultural, and aesthetic factors, with reason merely deferring to a particular causative factor rather than expressing the independent power of free will.

Oduwole appeals to the idea of the necessary complementary existence of both good and evil while grappling with the question of why an omnipotent God allows evil in the world. She uses complementary necessity with reference to the ordering of events in the world in a way that makes both good and evil complement each other (Oduwole 2007). She regards this complementarity as a dialectical relationship of good and evil. God is a perfect being, but he does not intervene to eradicate or reduce all or some of the evils in the world because doing so will affect the content of the goods in the world, perhaps by causing a drop in their quantity and quality. For Oduwole, evil sometimes is instrumental to a greater good, or what she calls the greatest good. The usefulness of evil indicates its dialectical relationship with good. In her words: 'The *kola*, though bitter to taste, has good medicinal qualities. Evil is thus necessary to the greatest good ... These problems [evils in the world] are all the manifestations of the deities and the machinations of evil forces in Yoruba cosmogony. Evil experiences are experiences that are relevant to the fullness of one's life' (Oduwole 2007, 12).

Oduwole does not clearly state what the greatest good is, but she seems to conflate it with the greater good, or a good compensatory state of affairs that follows from a connected evil state of affairs. Thus, she observes that a full life is made possible by the reality of evil in a world that offers many goods. However, the appeal to the necessity of a natural dialectical process does not cancel the reality of evil. Evil remains qualitatively different from good. The omnipotent and omniscient God that Oduwole presents in her discussion of traditional Yoruba religious thought is obliged to interfere with the good–evil dialectic in favour of the creation of, at least, more good than evil since he is also omnibenevolent. Indeed, the appeal to necessity and the dialectics of good and evil favours a metaphysical framework that argues for the existence of a limited God rather than a perfect God. Jonathan O. Chimakonam and Amara E. Chimakonam latch on to this intuition in their articulation of the idea of a harmony-God who sustains the balance of good and evil in the world, as I will show in Subsection 1.4.

The second conception of God in ATR presents God as limited in power, knowledge, and goodness. Early proponents of this view like Okot p'Bitek (1971) and Kwasi Wiredu (1992) radicalise the decolonisation perspective of early theistic scholars and assert that the latter did not go far enough in eliminating Western conceptual schemes from African religious scholarship. The limited God view has been defended by scholars like p'Bitek (1971, 2011), Chukwuemeka Nze (1981), Donatus Nwoga (1984), C. U. M. Ezekwugo (1987), and Kola Abimbola (2006). The majority of contemporary African philosophers of religion now favour the limited God view for reasons of its cultural rootedness and explanatory simplicity (see Sogolo 1993; Aja 1996; Bewaji 1998; Wiredu 1998, 2013; Oladipo 2004; Balogun 2009; Fayemi 2012; Agada 2022a, 2022b, 2023a; Chimakonam 2022; Cordeiro-Rodrigues and Agada 2022; Mosima 2022; Ojimba and Chidubem 2022; Attoe 2023; Chimakonam and Chimakonam 2023).

1.3 Introducing the Limitation Thesis

The limitation thesis diametrically opposes the transcendental, or perfect God, thesis. It states plainly that God is limited in power, knowledge, and goodness. Proponents of the limitation thesis hold nuanced views of God. Some are nontraditional theists to the extent that they regard God as a creator-deity or designer-deity who brings the world into being from the pre-existing resources of the universe conceived panentheistically as a totality that embraces all entities and relations, including God.[3] Prominent limited God theists include Wiredu, John Ayotunde I. Bewaji, Oladele A. Balogun, Ada Agada, Jonathan O. Chimakonam, Ademola K. Fayemi, and Luis Cordeiro-Rodrigues. Philosophers who may be grouped into the category of limited God non-theists are a tiny minority. p'Bitek (1971, 2011) and Attoe come readily to mind. The former presents a peculiar problem given that he sometimes presents the African God as a limited deity while consistently arguing that traditional African societies regard the limited God and other spiritual entities as not having objective existence, a stance that is undeniably atheistic. Attoe (2022a, 2022b) is the one philosopher who can be uncontroversially called a limited God non-theist, without any accompanying classificatory complication since he unambiguously presents God as an unconscious, depersonalised material entity without intelligent agency.

Proponents of the limitation thesis argue that traditional African societies do not attribute omnipotence, omniscience, and omnibenevolence to God, as earlier noted. They, more or less, favour the view that 'African peoples may describe their deities [including God] as "strong", but not "omnipotent"; "wise", but not "omniscient"; "old", not "eternal"; "great", not "omnipresent"' (p'Bitek 2011, 42). While p'Bitek demotes God to the rank of the pantheon of deities and divinities, most limited God proponents regard God as a kind of high deity to whom lesser deities are subordinated.[4] Limited God proponents point to African myths, proverbs, and world views to buttress the claim that God lacks the omni-properties. Wiredu, for example, supports his claim about God not being outside the world series by invoking the myth of the old woman who compelled God to move away from his first abode somewhere above the heads of human beings and go higher up into the sky to avoid being hit by the butt of the pestle with which the old woman was pounding food in a mortar (Wiredu 2013). He also references syntactic and semantic peculiarities of the Akan language to support his immanent conception of God. For him, the Akan language has no equivalent of the abstract existential English term 'to be' which implies that existence can be of an immaterial kind in addition to being of a material kind (Wiredu 1996, 49). To say something exists means this thing persists in a particular place. Since the Akan understanding of existence is always in a spatio-temporal sense, God must be spatio-temporal if he exists, according to Wiredu.

---

[3] Panentheism is broadly the view that God is interconnected with the world while remaining distinct from the world, such that changes and modifications in God affect other entities and vice versa (see, for example, Cordeiro-Rodrigues 2021; Agada 2022a).

[4] The polytheistic position held by p'Bitek is supported by Kola Abimbola (2006), who construes traditional Yoruba religion in a polytheistic way, with God, or Olodumare, being one member of a group of leading deities who compete with one another for supremacy.

Bewaji (1998) and Emmanuel Ofuasia (2022a) rely on the orally transmitted narratives of the Ifa Corpus of the Yoruba people while defending the limitation thesis. They point out that God sometimes solicits help from lesser deities and even human beings to complete certain tasks and gain certain knowledge about the world. The limitation thesis favours the idea of an eternally existing universe in which God emerges as the primordial being, with the most power and the highest knowledge of the mechanism of the universe. Although a powerful and knowledgeable being, God is not perfect since he is limited by the eternally existing universe whose resources he relies on to create or design worlds inhabited by far more limited beings, comparatively.

African philosophers of religion do not attempt to demonstrate the existence of the limited God by force of argument. Instead, they focus on the characterisation of God's relation with the world in ways that accommodate the reality of evil as a necessary dimension of an imperfect world. Such characterisation may be quasi-physicalist, as is the case with Wiredu, who conceives God as a spatio-temporally located entity who possesses unique powers of acting in ways not wholly explicable in the physicalist framework of current science. For example, God may behave like an immaterial entity not locatable in space and time, although he must be locatable in space and time if he must be deemed to actually exist. Philosophers like Agada, Motsamai Molefe (2018), Molefe and Mutshidzi Maraganedzha (2023), Chimakonam, Ofuasia, Cordeiro-Rodrigues, and Attoe conceive God in panpsychist, panentheistic, and materialistic terms. In the panpsychist perspective, God is regarded as a kind of cosmic mind, or the highest consciousness in the universe, who imparts his essence to all things in the universe without being himself a perfect being possessing the omni-properties. In the panentheistic perspective, God is regarded as an imperfect primordial being in an imperfect universe who is connected with entities in the universe in such a way that he is affected by modifications in the entities that he created. The materialistic understanding of God presents the primordial being as a mechanical cause of the world in the sense of being a necessary condition for the commencement of a mechanical interactive process that culminated in the emergence of diverse entities, some of which evolved consciousness and intelligence. The next section will explore the non-vitalist tradition of the limited God.

1.4 The Limited God in the Non-vitalist Tradition

The non-vitalist tradition avoids conceiving of God as a universal cosmic consciousness that animates entities in the universe with its essence or vital force. This tradition usually grants God creative agency and imbues him with sufficient power and knowledge that enable him to produce and order the world.

In this section, I will provide concise outlines of the characterisation of God's relation with the world in the works of Wiredu, Bewaji, Fayemi, Jonathan O. Chimakonam, Amara E. Chimakonam, and Attoe.

As a physicalist of the quasi-physicalist variety, Wiredu (1996, 1998, 2013) firmly believes that the universe is understandable within the framework of scientific knowledge, if not currently in a thorough manner, then at some future date when science must have advanced enough to fully account for quasi-physical phenomena like God that are believed to possess seemingly non-physical properties. Thus, quasi-physicalism proposes that while the universe is physical, some entities within it may behave in ways that current scientific knowledge cannot adequately account for (Wiredu 1996, 1998). With this postulation, Wiredu is able to account for traditional Akan belief in God, the soul, and spirits. For Wiredu, since the universe is physical, God is ultimately a physical entity.

However, Wiredu does not pursue the question of the material God's locatability in space and time. When he writes that the Akan conceive existence in a fundamentally empirical and spatio-temporal way, he rules out any possible location of God in some undifferentiated metaphysical space. This stance raises the question of where exactly the material God is located. Attoe (2022a) tries to respond to this question by vaguely identifying God with some physical constant like energy, as I will show later in this section. Nevertheless, Wiredu believes that the quasi-physical God is an imperfect entity in an imperfect world where physical evil exists necessarily and in which sentient and thinking beings like humans exhibit an inherent capacity for moral evil. God may be benevolent, but he cannot significantly tilt the good–evil balance in the world in favour of good because he is limited by the pre-existing physical stuff which he manipulates to design the world. Wiredu suggests that evil may have its origin in this primordial physical stuff given that it constitutes the foundation of entities in the universe. In his words:

> [The Akan] seem to operate with the notion of the power of God implying rather less than absolute omnipotence. That power is still unique in its extent, but it is conceptually not altogether unlike that of a human potentate. Indeed, God himself comes to be thought of as the model of a father who has laid well-intentioned plans for his children which are, however, sometimes impeded not only by their refractory wills but also by the grossness of the raw materials he has to work with. (Wiredu 1998, 41)

Bewaji (1998) and Fayemi (2012) find support for the limitation thesis in the Ifa Corpus and the traditional Yoruba belief system. The Ifa Corpus frequently narrates events that suggest that God, or Olodumare, is limited in power, knowledge, and goodness. For example, God consults lesser deities and even human beings in his quest for eternal existence and the acquisition of knowledge of future events (Bewaji 1998; Fayemi 2012; see also Agada 2022a; Ofuasia 2022a). The duo readily concede that God is the highest being in the universe, the creator of lesser deities and the world. His attributes are of a very high order, without reaching the level expected of a perfect being. For Bewaji:

> [T]he fact that some things happen 'behind His back' or 'without His direct awareness' has been borne out in the practical aspects of creation, sustenance, and running of the universe, here, there, and everywhere, including even the domain of Olodumare (Orun or heaven). He [God] has had recourse to the use of Orunmila and Ifa, the wise ones and the means of discerning the situation of things past, present, and future. (Bewaji 1998, 8)

Fayemi observes that:

> *Olodumare* delegated power to some deities in order to accomplish the task of creation. The universe and everything in it were created by the joint efforts of *Olodumare* and his divinities. Thus, while *Olodumare* is the primary cause of events and occurrences, the activities of the lesser gods or divinities (called Orisas) constitute the important secondary causes. (Fayemi 2012, 7)

In accordance with the limitation thesis, Bewaji and Fayemi regard evil as a necessary phenomenon of the universe which God himself is capable of inflicting on entities in the world. Since he is not omniscient, he could not have predicted the occurrence of some future evils at the time he created the world and, not being omnipotent, he could not eliminate the evil that he was aware of at the time of creation; not being omnibenevolent, he himself could contribute his share of the quantity and variety of evil in the world. However, since God possesses substantial power and knowledge and since he is overall good, he may be aware of his moral obligation to at least reduce some of the evils in the world, even if he cannot eliminate them. One may point out that the concept of limitation entails incapacity. If God is limited, then he is unable to reduce the evil in the world. However, limitation does not equate to absolute incapacity since God expresses his power in degrees even if this power is not of the order of omnipotence. Thus, the limited God may be aware of certain current evils and be able to carry out remedial actions that reduce the intensity of these evils. Fayemi (2012, 12) especially holds this view of a limited but morally responsible creator (cf. Agada 2023a; Cordeiro-Rodrigues 2023). For Fayemi, the limited God can be blamed for the existence of physical and spiritual evils that cannot be attributed to human moral agency (Fayemi 2012, 12). He brings evils inflicted by invisible spiritual entities under the category of spiritual evil. If the limited God is conceived as an entity that creates *ex materia*, one must concede that he is indeed very powerful and should be able to eliminate some of the evils in the world.

Chimakonam and Chimakonam (2023) approach the question of a limited God from a complementaristic metaphysical framework that favours the view that the universe is an interconnected totality where seemingly opposing entities and variables complement each other. The positing of complementarity makes the existence of things necessary. A thing exists for itself and for other entities in such an interconnected way that it not existing will fundamentally alter the state of the universe. This is the case because the complementary universe maintains a harmonious balance of qualities and relations. In this interconnected, complementary universe, God becomes a harmony-God whose grandeur lies precisely in the fact that he is able to maintain the harmony in the universe. For the Chimakonams, as powerful and knowledgeable as the harmony-God is, he is not omnipotent and omniscient because his essence reflects the imperfect nature of the universe. Both good and evil necessarily coexist. The elimination of evil will mean the elimination of good. The most a harmony-God can do about the quantity and quality of evils in the world is reduce evils in such a way that the good–evil balance is sustained. Thus, if God does not (or cannot) prevent a devastating earthquake from occurring in Turkey, he averts an equally devastating wildfire in California or increases the seasonal harvests in Nigeria in a way that perfectly compensates for the human suffering in Turkey, in the cosmic context. In the Chimakonams' words:

> He brings the rain, but also brings the sun. He raises a forest only to blaze it down with fire. He gives a child to a mother and takes it the next day. He creates and destroys not just for the fun of it but for the overarching need to maintain the balance of good and evil. (Chimakonam and Chimakonam 2023, 334)

They add that:

> Imperfection is one of the most important features of the world . . . God would not exist in and for a morally perfect universe. If He existed, He would not be conceivable. If He is conceivable, he would not be God, at least, for us because he would not command the awe and worship of any human . . . If the world were perfect, humans would be perfect. No one would have the senses of imperfection, lack, and need that make the idea of God relevant. (334)

They assert that in an imperfect universe, only a harmony-God can exist. A harmony-God 'is one who has the capacity for the opposing values of good and evil, and represents a being in whom both polar values complement each other' (334). While it can be argued that consciousness of an imperfect world would rather incline human beings to conceive a worship-worthy God as one who is perfect rather than limited, the Chimakonams make a significant point about the empirical correlation between an imperfect world and its imperfect creator, although they do not attempt to produce an elaborate teleological or cosmological argument for the existence of the limited God.

Attoe (2022a) builds on Wiredu's idea of a quasi-physical God and proposes the existence of a thoroughly material God who is a material first cause. His unconscious God is a material first cause in an interconnected universe in the sense of serving as the necessary condition for the commencement of a rigidly deterministic sequence of events that culminates in the emergence of a world such as ours. Attoe does not show clearly whether the unconscious God is contemporaneous with the universe, whether this God predates or post-dates it, or whether God or the universe is beginningless, but he firmly asserts that God lacks intelligent agency. Attoe's conception of God indicates radical limitation since God does not act intentionally. The impotence of Attoe's God renders his first material cause appellation for God an ironic one (cf. Chimakonam and Chimakonam 2023). This is the case because Attoe's God is not a conscious, rational agent but a mere mechanical principle of the world. Faced with the question of the location of the material God that Wiredu did not adequately answer, Attoe suggests that what we call God may simply be a dimension of a physical constant like energy. He notes:

> The concept of God ... need not be that of a personalized deity, so I refer to God as an It (expressing it as neuter or non-gendered). Since my idea of God is not spiritual or otherworldly, and since I showed that it was necessary for God to be an existent thing for reality to be, my very simple concept of God could only view It as a material being, and I often wondered whether enduring things like energy could not be an aspect of what I called God. (Attoe 2022a, 8)

Attoe's response to the question of the material God's location in space and time is a hesitant response. He hesitates because he is aware of the atheistic implication of connecting God's existence with a physical constant which may have no objective reality, after all, outside the theoretical explanatory framework of science. In dodging the atheistic implication of his conception of God as an unconscious material principle, Attoe fares no better than Wiredu in accounting for the location of the material God. Unsurprisingly, Attoe's God is neither responsible for the evil in the world nor obliged to reduce it. This God is, after all, an unconscious entity.[5]

---

[5] Indeed, Attoe denies the objective reality of evil. For him, what humans call evil is merely an anthropomorphic projection of our opinions about unfavourable states of affairs. In the next subsection, I will provide outlines of the vitalist tradition of the limitation thesis.

1.5 The Limited God in the Vitalist Tradition

The vitalist tradition typically conceives God in panpsychist and panentheistic ways. Panpsychism is broadly the view that mind or mind-stuff is fundamental and distributed throughout the world while panentheism is the view that God is interconnected with the world such that he affects the world and is affected by the world. God is represented either as a cosmic consciousness who distributes a vitalistic quality in the world (Molefe 2018; Agada 2022b, 2023a; Cordeiro-Rodrigues and Agada 2022; Molefe and Maraganedzha 2023) or as the being who best exemplifies the vitalistic and creative essence that animates the universe (Agada 2015, 2022b; Ofuasia 2022a). Placide Tempels is regarded as the front runner of vitalism in African philosophy. I leave him out of the limited God vitalist tradition because his discussion of God as the source of vital force in the universe is consistent with the stance of traditional theism. Tempels' idea of God as a maximal entity who perfectly embodies vital force and as the source of this quality presents God as the supreme being in the universe that he created (see Tempels 1959). While he does not argue this point, the traditional theistic perspective dominates Tempels' interpretation of traditional Bantu thought.

Classifying Molefe as a limited God vitalist thinker or a traditional theistic vitalist proponent is not quite a straightforward exercise given that Molefe does not focus effort on the articulation of God's nature. However, he is aware of the fact that his identification of God as the source and distributor of vital force, or vitality, may be amenable to either a traditional theistic or limited God characterisation. Reflecting on his conception of God as the supreme epitome of vitality, Molefe observes that:

> This understanding of God as essentially characterised by vitality has interesting implications for theology and morality. It presents a fresh perspective to religious ethical systems. Typical systems conceive of God as … (all) powerful, knowing and loving. This African ontological system [vitality-based conception of God] conceives of God as chiefly characterised by life, and the cosmos that he created partakes and is also characterised by this life force. (Molefe 2018, 27)

Molefe's non-endorsement of traditional theism tempts me to tentatively group him with the limited God theists of the vitalist tradition. Once one conceives vitality as an imperfect animating quality, it becomes much easier to lump Molefe with limited God theists. This vitalistic God may not be omnipotent, omniscient, and omnibenevolent, but he is powerful and knowledgeable enough to create the world and good enough to want to increase the vital force of human beings. Increasing human vital force will entail reducing the evils and suffering in the world. But can a limited God reduce the suffering in the world? Molefe's promotion of moral living in terms of more life, or heightened liveliness, indicates that humans actually act in ways that reduce suffering in the world. If humans have the ability to reduce suffering, then God, who is more life-filled and lively than humans, can also work to reduce suffering in the world. Whether God can eliminate suffering is a different question. As long as one is interpreting Molefe as a limited God theist, his vitalistic God cannot eliminate evil from the world.

Ofuasia conceives God in a panentheistic way, drawing inspiration from traditional Yoruba religious thought and the process theology of Alfred North Whitehead (1978). From traditional Yoruba thought, Ofuasia (2022a, 2022b) borrows the idea of the interconnection and interdependence of divinity and humanity and from Whitehead, he borrows the idea of a fundamental vitalistic principle that animates the universe and may well predate even God. Whitehead calls this fundamental principle creativity, in which inheres the metaphysical laws of the universe. It animates God and other entities although God better exemplifies it (Whitehead 1978). It is as the highest exemplar of creativity that God can be understood as simultaneously a product of creativity and its condition. While God is constituted by creativity, he has the highest knowledge of this principle and can manipulate it in his capacity as an orderer in an evolutionary universe oriented towards novelty.

In applying the concept of creativity to African philosophical theology, Ofuasia (2022a, 95) defines it as 'that primordial ground on which all things, God included, thrive'. If God is preceded by creativity and bound by the metaphysical laws of the universe that are inherent in creativity, then God is limited. He can do a vast number of things but not everything. His knowledge is of a great order indeed but not in the range of omniscience. Ofuasia supports his view with evidence extracted from the Ifa Corpus, where it is clearly narrated that God the creator also depends on what he has created to reach a higher level of power and knowledge. God collaborates with lesser deities to govern the world and consults deities and humans when he is faced with great puzzles (Ofuasia 2022b). Consequently, God cannot eliminate evil. The evil that exists in the world will appear to be a necessary consequence of an imperfect universe that is continuing to evolve and whose final form cannot be predicted by any entity. Going by Ofuasia's understanding of God, the deity can be deemed knowledgeable enough to know the truth value of most but not all propositions.

In the thought of Cordeiro-Rodrigues (2021), panentheism and panpsychism are presented as frameworks that best explain the nature of God in African thought. For him, God is the highest consciousness in the universe, the distributor of vital force. He is affected by changes in entities and the world, being the distributor of vital force that connects his essence with all things in the world. If the world is imperfect and modifications within it affect God, then God himself is imperfect, more or less. God, as conceived by Cordeiro-Rodrigues, is a relational entity. But his limitation does not follow merely from his mutability; instead, the crucial factor is the vital force itself. While Cordeiro-Rodrigues does not go far enough to argue that the vital force embodies imperfection, he yet suggests that this may be the case since vital force is the animating principle of a world that clearly exhibits moral and physical evil.

1.6 The Limited Consolation God

I have argued in a number of works that the limiting principle in the universe must be sought in the animating principle, what Wiredu calls the pre-existing stuff and what Ofuasia prefers to label creativity, following Whitehead (see Agada 2015, 2022a, 2022b, 2023a). African philosophers like Molefe and Martin Nkemnkia (1999) and Western scholars who work on African philosophy like Tempels and Cordeiro-Rodrigues label the animating principle vital force or life force, or simply vitality. I labelled the universal animating principle *mood* and offered for the first time in the literature an explanation of the limiting propensity of the animating principle (see Section 3.2). I observed elsewhere that: '*Mood* . . . is the yearning of eternity. The human mood is a reflection of the mood of the universe. The human mood exhibits the complexities of the constituents of existence which once apprehended we call feelings, precisely joy and sadness' (Agada 2015, 25). It is 'the primordial mind-matter interface and the source of all intelligence and emotions in the universe' (Agada 2022b, 87).

Mood is the yearning of eternity in the sense that it is the essence of all things and is expressed in all things as yearning. In the human being, *mood* is readily grasped through our understanding of the emotions of joy and sadness, which provide a measure of the human mind's optimistic and pessimistic states. The more joyful a sentient and rational being is, the more optimistic it becomes. The sadder this being is, the more pessimistic it becomes. Optimism and pessimism highlight the question of the worth of human existence and the point, or pointlessness, of the universe. *Mood* as an event, an animating principle, is neither wholly immaterial nor wholly material. It is yearning, and it expresses itself in all things as yearning. Given its yearning essence, *mood* is incomplete and imperfect. Whatever it animates exhibits incompleteness (see Section 3.2.1). Accordingly, God is imperfect, for he is animated by *mood*. He is a consolation God from the perspective of consolationism. Just as the universe yearns in perpetuity for completeness without ever reaching this state, so does God yearn for perfection without ever attaining the omni-properties. He is called a consolation God because, notwithstanding his lack of the omni-properties, he is sufficiently powerful and knowledgeable to create an imperfect world which he seeks to make better within the limit of imperfection (see Section 3.2.3).

The concept of *mood* is articulated in the context of the philosophy of consolationism. This philosophy acknowledges the fact that the world clearly exhibits characteristics of imperfection as prominently exemplified by the reality of moral and physical evil. Moral evil encompasses harm caused by the informed actions of sentient and intelligent entities like human beings while physical evil indicates harm brought about by events necessitated by the imperfect structure of the world which are either wholly or largely beyond human control (Agada 2015, 2022b). An example of moral evil is murder while a typical example of physical evil is a devastating earthquake. The harmful actions of a mentally challenged person that lead to the death of someone can also be regarded as a physical evil since the real culprit in this case is a natural phenomenon, a disability.

Consolationism asserts that an evolutionary universe such as ours produces both good and evil as *mood* actualises itself in the search for a more complete state of being. Accordingly, the essence of *mood* is yearning. But since yearning indicates being in a perpetual process of becoming, the motivating goal of perfection cannot be reached. Consolationism therefore describes an eternal universe with a tragic dimension given that the goal of perfection is indicated even as it is unachievable. Good and evil are products of the yearning essence, or *mood*. In the consolationist system, God is called the eternal mood of melancholy in the sense that he is a possible entity who has the most knowledge of the operation of *mood* and the most power to manipulate it. The invocation of the notion of melancholy immediately discloses the idea that God has emotions. Melancholy in the consolationist system refers to the sentient and thinking being's condition as a yearning, imperfect entity in search of consolation, that which increases the state of joy and diminishes sadness. Consolation can also be understood as a state of mind in which emotional and intellectual satisfaction are derived from the knowledge of events that cause or can enhance the state of joy (Agada 2022b, 63). Melancholy therefore is not a mere negative term understood in terms of great sadness but connotes the dialectic of joy and sadness. The idea of a possible God will be discussed in greater detail in Section 3 of this Element.

But God is not *mood* nor the source of *mood* although he represents the fullest development of *mood* and is indeed a being of great power and knowledge. I note elsewhere that *mood* is:

> The primordial mind-matter interface, the necessary and fundamental unity in which mind and matter originate. Since *mood* is now conceived as a yearning

essence or power in the universe, immanent and dialectical, it can neither be wholly mentalistic nor wholly material. *Mood* is a proto-mind given that it is an event rather than a strictly material or strictly immaterial phenomenon. The 'mind' qualification merely underlines the eventist framework in which *mood* is articulated. (Agada 2022b, 66)

The yearning essence of *mood* and the perpetual transgressing of its mind–matter boundary makes possible the production of the novelty Ofuasia writes about. The emergence of worlds, entities, good, and evil are some of the novelties which yearning expresses. God is the highest expression of *mood*. He is, however, limited by this same principle that constitutes his being since limitation is the nature of yearning. That which yearns seeks the overcoming of an inherent lack. This lack is an active dimension of limitation. The limited *mood* expresses a limited God who creates the world from the resources of *mood* that are available in the universe. God creates precisely because he is sufficiently knowledgeable and powerful to accomplish the task of creation. But he is neither omnipotent nor omniscient. He is benevolent but not omnibenevolent (Agada 2023a). In the consolationist system, evil is a real but negative dimension of yearning: negative in the sense of causing harm to entities that exist as necessary expressions of *mood*.

1.7 Conclusion

This section introduced the reader to the African philosophy of religion literature, with a focus on how African philosophers have characterised God's relation with the world. I noted that there is a traditional theistic conception of God in the literature that presents God as a perfect being who possesses the omni-properties and contrasted this conception of God with the limited God view that denies God possession of the omni-properties. I explored the limited God literature and highlighted the vitalist and non-vitalist traditions of the limited God view. In the next section, I will critically discuss the implications of the limited God view for the problem of evil in continuation of the exploration of the literature.

2 The Limitation Thesis and the Problem of Evil
2.1 Introduction

In this section, I focus on the characterisation of the relation between the limited God and evil in the literature. I explore the concepts of power, knowledge, and goodness and the extent of the limited God's incapacity. I supply a global context for the limitation thesis and raise the question of the logical and evidential problem of evil from the perspective of African philosophy of religion. The section critically examines the positions of a number of limited God theists as well as the non-theist stance of Aribiah Attoe. The section concludes with the suggestion that while the limited God is not the cause of evil and cannot eliminate it, he can be deemed morally responsible for the evil in the world in his creative capacity. This suggestion sets the agenda for an in-depth discussion of the limited God's moral responsibility in Section 3.

2.2 On the Categories of Power, Knowledge, and Goodness

Traditional theism in the Judaic, Christian, and Islamic traditions presents God as a perfect being, for the most part. As a perfect being, God is not merely powerful but omnipotent, not just knowledgeable but omniscient, and not simply good but omnibenevolent. God's possession of the omni-properties involves the question of capacity. God is able to do all (logically possible) things. He is able to know all things and able to love completely in a way that rules out deficiencies like malice and malevolence.

This understanding of God naturally inspires questions about why the perfect God allows the magnitude and varieties of evil in the world. Philosophers have reflected on omnipotence and evil for centuries. Epicurus, the ancient Greek philosopher, raised the problem of evil in the world in relation to the existence of a perfect God when he wondered whether God is indeed omnipotent and omnibenevolent (see Hume [1777] 2007, 73). For Epicurus, if God is willing to prevent evil but cannot actually do so, he must be limited. If he is able but not willing, he is not benevolent. But if he is both able and willing to prevent evil, then we are faced with a puzzle. Theists in the Western tradition have attempted to solve the puzzle by constructing theodicies and defences of theism in the face of evil in the world. The free will and greater good argument, soul-making theodicy, and sceptical theism are some of the best-known defences of trad-itional theism (see, for example, Plantinga 1965; Wykstra 1984; Stump 1985; Alston 1991; Swinburne 1998; Bergmann 2009; cf. Sterba 2019). While an in-depth discussion of Western theodicies is beyond the scope of this Element, I will briefly highlight problems with these theodicies in Section 2.3 to provide the broadest possible context for the African limited God thesis.

In contrast to the perfect God vision of the dominant conceptions of God in Judaism, Christianity, and Islam, a dominant conception of God in ATR pre-sents the deity as limited in power, knowledge, and goodness (see Section 1.2). The limited African God may lack the fullness of power, knowledge, and goodness, but he is by no means powerless (see Bewaji 1998; Fayemi 2012; Cordeiro-Rodrigues 2021; Agada 2022a, 2022b; Chimakonam 2022; Cordeiro-Rodrigues and Agada 2022; Gwara and Ogbonnaya 2022; Chimakonam and

Chimakonam 2023; Cordeiro-Rodrigues 2023). The following representative quotes from a number of African philosophers of religion help in the task of delineating the scope of the limited God's power.

Reflecting on traditional Akan religious thought, Wiredu observes:

> Though in the context of cosmological reflection, they [Akan people] maintain a doctrine of unqualified omnipotence, in connection with issues having a direct bearing on the fate of humankind on this earth, such as the problem of evil, they seem to operate with a notion of the power of God implying rather less than absolute omnipotence. That power is still unique in its extent, but it is conceptually not altogether unlike that of a human potentate. (Wiredu 1998, 41)

Wiredu is saying that, in theory, there is the temptation to make sweeping statements about God's excellence and attribute properties like omnipotence to him. Wiredu suggests that the Akan are guilty of making such imputations. He notes, however, that questions raised by practical issues such as the problem of evil compel further reflection on the magnitude of God's excellence. Second thought persuades the Akan that not only is God not omnipotent, but also that his power may be better understood by drawing analogies with the power of a king. A human potentate may wield great power indeed, but they cannot do everything humanly possible, let alone all things logically possible.

While noting that the Yoruba regard God as limited in power and knowledge, Bewaji concedes that God is still the most powerful entity in the world. Bewaji notes thus:

> The evidence that Olodumare is the creator of everything is displayed in virtually all accounts of the relationship between Olodumare and the Universe. Where He did not directly cause or create, He instructed the divinities to create and He supervised the creation work. So, he created both the good and the bad, the well-formed and the deformed, the rainy season and the drought. Through Him must be sought the cause of all things. And everything there is has a rationale and can be understood and used by the thoughtful and gifted like the herbalists and medicine men. (Bewaji 1998, 8)

Bewaji describes a limited God who is yet very powerful and knowledgeable. This God creates either directly through the immediate exercise of his powers or indirectly through lesser deities under his control.

Fayemi observes that:

> *Olodumare* or Eleda is seen by the Yoruba as the ultimate cause of all visible processes in the world. By being the creator, it does not mean that He unilaterally creates everything without the support of and consultation with other divinities … *Olodumare* delegated power to some deities in order to

accomplish the task of creation. The universe and everything in it were created by the joint efforts of *Olodumare* and his divinities. Thus, while *Olodumare* is the primary cause of events and occurrences, the activities of the lesser gods or divinities (called Orisas) constitute the important secondary causes. (Fayemi 2012, 7)

Fayemi's stance does not radically deviate from Bewaji's view. However, Fayemi grants God less power. For Fayemi, the lesser deities play a more active role in the process of creation. They actively assist God as co-creators, even if in a subordinate capacity.

Jonathan O. Chimakonam and Amara E. Chimakonam assert that:

There is no empirical proof to date of any devout whose life has been made whole. A harmony-God is one who has the capacity for the opposing values of good and evil, and represents a being in whom both polar values complement each other. To those who worship Him, He rewards good deeds with good, and punishes bad ones with evil. He brings the rain, but also brings the sun. He raises a forest only to blaze it down with fire. He gives a child to a mother and takes it the next day. He creates and destroys not just for the fun of it but for the overarching need to maintain the balance of good and evil. What is the point of having so much power if you would not use it? He is the harmony-God, and His ultimate concern is to balance the use of his good and evil relational capacities, which is what makes Him command the awe and worship of humans who could not sustain such a balance. (Chimakonam and Chimakonam 2023, 334)

The maintenance of harmony in the world indicates the extent of the power wielded by the harmony-God described by the Chimakonams. In maintaining the good–evil balance, the harmony-God sustains the cosmic order. Only a very powerful and knowledgeable entity can perform the harmony-sustaining task. The Chimakonams introduce an interesting angle to the debate about the scope of the limited God's power when they assert that the raison d'etre of God's existence is the sustenance of the harmony in the world. Accordingly, God is properly the harmony-God. While not possessing the omni-properties, he is yet a very powerful being. For a being to so order the world that there is a perpetual balance of good and evil and other seemingly opposed variables means that this being is a very powerful entity, and no doubt the most powerful being in the specific world or universe where he operates. Yet this very powerful being is not omnipotent, according to the Chimakonams, because the world created by this being manifests imperfection. If God was perfect, he would have created a perfect world. They reject the subtlety of Western theodicies and assert that the imperfect character of the world provides an insurmountable conceptual obstacle for any kind of theodicy.

There are two possible objections to the Chimakonams' account which I will briefly discuss. One may point out that there is no harmony in the world, only a semblance of order. One may also object to the claim that a limited being can sustain the harmony in the world if, for the sake of argument, it is granted that there is indeed harmony in the world. The first objection distinguishes between order and harmony. Order implies regularity while harmony implies both regularity and the perfection of regular phenomena. That is to say, while order indicates predictability and uniformity, harmony demands the perfection or completeness of the parts that work together to produce the quality of predictability and uniformity. The Chimakonams may respond by insisting that the objector is conceiving harmony in teleological terms, in terms of a grand cosmic purpose, while they understand harmony in horizontal terms that reference worldly projects that can be completed. The emphasis is not only on quality but also quantity, since the world is already acknowledged as imperfect. Thus one may say that harmony has been realised if the death of an old man in one country is balanced by the birth of a child in a different country. The second objection is a more stubborn one because it challenges the claim that a limited God can sustain harmony in the world.

According to the Chimakonams, evil exists necessarily in a complementary universe. The limited harmony-God can neither eliminate nor prevent evil, although he can do good and evil. Indeed, his task is not preventing evil but ensuring that the evil in the world does not outweigh the good in the world at a particular time.[6] If God cannot prevent evil in the world, it is difficult to see how he can sustain the good–evil balance in the world in a way that guarantees harmony given the variety and magnitude of good and evil events in the world. If he intervenes in location B to reduce or increase good or evil in order to restore balance that has been qualitatively and quantitatively disturbed in location A, he has not actually prevented evil. He has merely maintained the overall good–evil balance in the world. But it is not clear how his limited power can bring about a precise correspondence between all the kinds and degrees of good and evil in the world in all locations.

While acknowledging God's limitation and the seemingly ubiquitous influence of lesser deities, Olusegun Oladipo stresses the great powers that God wields. Oladipo writes that traditional African societies often regard God as:

[T]he maker of the world and its sustainer and ruler; the origin and giver of life who is above all divinities and man; a supreme judge and a controller of human destiny. These attributes show that the Supreme Being in African

---

[6] If the harmony-God does prevent evil in order to maintain the good–evil balance, then the Chimakonams have not clarified the matter yet.

> cultures is regarded as the ultimate reality ... the Supreme Being, called
> *Onyame* by the Akans, *Chukwu* by the Igbos, and *Olodumare* by the Yorubas,
> to cite a few examples, can be regarded as the ultimate point of reference in
> whatever may be called African traditional religion. (Oladipo 2004, 357)

For Oladipo, God occupies a position of supremacy relative to other entities. He sustains and controls the world. His conception of God is similar to Bewaji's and Fayemi's conceptions of the deity. Bewaji, Fayemi, and Oladipo stress the fact that the limited God is not powerless when they call him a creator. He cannot do everything logically possible, but he can do a great many things that the lesser deities and humans cannot do.

While Emmanuel Ofuasia (2022a, 89) admits that 'reality is a product of the collaboration between Olodumare [God] and the divinities that in the end underscores *creatio ex materia*', he stresses that the divinities are subordinate to God. For Ofuasia, God is the entity with the fullest measure of being and therefore the most powerful. However, the divine power is not of the order of omnipotence since God depends on the world as much as the world depends on him. Ofuasia supports his panentheistic conception of God with references to the Ifa Corpus of the Yoruba, which often narrates how God consults lesser deities and human heroes when he is puzzled over certain phenomena. Drawing on process metaphysics, Ofuasia asserts that God's agency is of a passive kind, consistent with his limitedness. For him, passive agency involves God acting persuasively and in cooperation with creatures to actualise his plans for the world. For him, it is a being who possesses the attributes of omnipotence and omniscience who can act coercively, through the imposition of divine fiats on the world.

Attoe's non-theistic stance, as noted in Section 1, denies God agency completely. Accordingly, God is not a being to which the categories of power, knowledge, and goodness apply. However, Attoe's stance is unique. For the majority of limited God proponents, God possesses intelligence, will, and personality. Since the limited God cannot do everything logically possible, his knowledge and goodness are limited. He is knowledgeable enough to understand the best way to wield his power, but he is not omniscient. He is good enough to wish a measure of meaningful existence for entities like the human being whom he created, but, not being all-loving, he can overlook the suffering of human beings and focus on the improvement of his own condition. I will return to this matter in Section 3. In the next subsection, I will briefly discuss the problem of evil in the world as it features in Western analytic philosophy of religion with the goal of providing a broad context for the African engagement with the problem of evil.

2.3 The Problem of Evil

In this section, I will use the term *evil* to indicate harm and suffering as it exists in the world. I categorise evil into moral and physical evil. Moral evil indicates harm and suffering caused by creaturely wickedness. Human beings and deities are examples of entities with the capacity for creaturely wickedness. Physical evil is harm and suffering caused by natural phenomena such as earthquakes, hurricanes, epidemics, and torrential rainfall. Moral evil consists of premeditated actions like murder, theft, cruelty, torture, and so on.

Traditional theism, and Christian theism in particular, attributes perfection to God. The problem of evil follows from the basic premises of traditional theism, which claims that there exists an omnipotent, omniscient, and omnibenevolent creator of the world. If this assertion is true, can there be a morally justifiable reason for God allowing the scale and variety of evil one encounters in the world? The problem is usually formulated in two ways, with both formulations interlocking since the reality of evil in the world is assumed in both cases. We have, on the one hand, the logical problem and, on the other hand, the evidential problem. The logical problem states that the idea of a perfect God seems incompatible with the reality of evil in the world. The evidential problem suggests that the variety, magnitude, and intensity of evil in the world raise the probability that the perfect God of the traditional theist does not exist.

Theistic philosophers like John Hick, Alvin Plantinga, Richard Swinburne, Eleonore Stump, and Stephen J. Wykstra have responded to the problem of evil by proposing and/or modifying the soul-making, free will, and sceptical theistic arguments in the face of sustained critique of traditional theism. According to the soul-making argument proposed by Hick (1966), suffering enables humans to acquire morally worthy virtues like courage, compassion, tolerance, and patience which prepare them for union with God in heaven, where evil does not exist. Accordingly, evil is not a pointless phenomenon; it is required for the actualisation of a greater good. One obvious criticism of the soul-making argument is that people can acquire the qualities Hick references without evil existing or occurring (see, for example, Kane 1975, 2). One can acquire the virtues of patience and tolerance through having to deal with a troublesome toddler, for example. The time invested in caring, providing close supervision, enduring the incessant childish whims, and calming screaming sessions may very well instil patience in a parent in a manner that manifests positively in the parent's wider social interactions. An emotionally or physically debilitating experience, which we call suffering, does not have to occur for the virtues of patience and tolerance to be gained.

Plantinga advances the free will defence in an attempt to invalidate the logical problem of evil, which emphasises the conceptual inconsistency of the proposition that a perfect God exists and is the creator of a world with plenty of evils. He accepts that humans have free will and that free will is a great good. This capacity enables humans to voluntarily choose to do good rather than evil. Therefore, it is a valuable good, the possession of which outweighs all the evil in the world (Plantinga 1965, 204–220). God is morally justified in permitting moral evil to safeguard the good of free will. But how does Plantinga approach physical evil? Like the African theist Kwame Gyekye, who attributes physical evil to the free actions of malevolent spirits (see Section 1.2), Plantinga suggests tentatively that natural evil may be accounted for by the free choices of Satan and his fallen angels which God safeguards at the cost of allowing evil. It is not within God's power to create a world where there is a greater 'balance of good over evil with respect to the actions of the nonhuman persons it contains' (Plantinga 1977, 58). He assumes that the phenomenon of evil is broadly a moral type, with narrowly moral and physical evils being species of the 'broadly moral evil' (59). The basic intuition is that evil enters the world through the free actions of intelligent agents, human or non-human. How suffering caused by an earthquake, for example, can be adequately accounted for in terms of Plantinga's broad moral evil is, of course, a legitimate question. A discussion of the matter is, however, beyond the scope of this Element.

To meet the objection that an omnipotent, omniscient, and omnibenevolent God who values human free will as a great good can prevent evil by preventing situations under which evil occurs while preserving free will, Plantinga adds the idea of transworld depravity to his free will defence. It seems that the free-willing human being may will the commission of a crime and fail to actually commit the crime because God removes the exact condition necessary for the willed evil to occur. Plantinga imagines possible worlds where a person performs only morally worthy actions. He then observes that in every possible world, there is a morally significant action that will deviate from the norm (the performance of only moral actions) if the situation or circumstances of the action took place in the actual world. In every possible world, there is a segment of it that is neutral with regard to a person performing or not performing a morally significant action. According to Plantinga, if that segment was in the actual world, the person would fail the moral test – that is, they would do wrong (Plantinga 1977, 48). Plantinga's contention is that God cannot create a world with only good and no evil because persons suffer from transworld depravity. Obviously, the idea of transworld depravity will pose no problem for an African limited God theist since the limitation thesis asserts that all persons in all possible worlds suffer from transworld depravity because evil necessarily exists, such that even God does not escape the necessity.

For Plantinga, the idea of a perfect God who possesses the omni-properties is compatible with the reality of evil. However, the plausibility of the free will defence has been called into question. Steve Boer has noted that God granting the good of free will does not mean that humans will always be able to actualise the evil that they will, since God can intervene either naturally or miraculously to thwart evildoers and prevent the harm intended by the free-willed act (cited in Stump 1985, 394). The point is that free will can be safeguarded without the actual occurrence of evil. It may be that the idea of transworld depravity adequately responds to Boer's objection, but it is not clear that the thesis of transworld depravity is true (see Otte 2009, 166). Recently, James P. Sterba (2019) has denied that there is actually a free will defence, as far as one is talking about the kind of freedom that exists in the world. For him, the moral evil in the world cannot be explained away by invoking the freedom that the world provides to creatures. He deploys the concept of significant freedom, as distinct from Plantinga's libertarian or absolute freedom, which he reinvents in the context of the political philosophy of the just state. In a just state, what should be safeguarded is not an absolute freedom but, rather, a significant freedom that guarantees the interests of all persons. A significant freedom is a basic right, the deprivation of which negatively affects the flourishing of the individual. A police officer acts morally when she restricts the less significant freedom of a man set to assault his partner in order to protect the more significant freedom of the partner. Going by libertarian freedom, the would-be attacker has the freedom to assault, but the partner has a more significant freedom not to be assaulted (Sterba 2019, 14). A God possessing the omni-properties ought to intervene or be sufficiently involved in the world to prevent evils that deprive victims of their significant freedom. The heart of the matter is not God creating creatures and giving them free will. In his words:

> [T]he real problem comes later in time when God fails to restrict the lesser freedoms of wrongdoers to secure the more significant freedoms of their victims ... there is much that God could have done to promote freedom by restricting freedom that simply has not been done. So we cannot say that God's justification for permitting the moral evil in the world is the freedom that is in it because God could have reduced the moral evil in the world by increasing the significant freedom in the world. (Sterba 2019, 29)

Swinburne builds on the stances of Hick and Plantinga in his own response to the problem of evil. Like Plantinga, he asserts that humans possess free will and like Hick, he links character formation to the evil in the world. However, he insists that it is not the bare fact of free will that matters but its *significant* exercise (see Swinburne 1998).[7] He emphasises what he calls efficacious free will, rather than Plantinga's libertarian free will, to underline the destiny-shaping effects of human choices, how people's decisions instigate or prevent serious evils in the world (17). The free will that God gives us enables us to be useful. It is, therefore, a freedom more desirable than a toy freedom that God could have given us in a world with significantly less suffering than ours but also with significantly less freedom (248). Given that on balance, a person's life is often a good one and death happens to ensure suffering does not become excessive, given that free will is a great good and in view of the reward that awaits one in the afterlife, God has a right to allow suffering in the world, according to Swinburne.

Today, many Western analytic philosophers of religion agree that Plantinga's free will defence responds adequately to the logical problem of evil by showing that the concept of omnipotence and the notion of evil in the world are compatible. The free will defence, broadly construed, is less successful in addressing the evidential problem of evil, which presents the more immediate and practical issue of the variety and magnitude of evil in the world. According to William Rowe (1979, 336), the world presents us with instances of great suffering that an omnipotent, omniscient, and omnibenevolent God could have prevented without, in the process, sacrificing a greater good or allowing an evil state just as bad or worse than the prevailing evil state. The evils implicated in this sort of suffering are gratuitous evils. The point is that it appears that if a perfect God exists, he ought not to permit evil to achieve his purpose if he can actualise this purpose without allowing the evil. Therefore, it seems improbable that the God of traditional theism exists.

Sceptical theism has been proposed as a good response to the evidential problem. It asserts that given the limited cognitive equipment of human beings, evil necessarily retains a mysterious aspect. God may have morally justifiable reasons for permitting evil in the world which we are, unfortunately, unable to access given our limited cognitive faculty (see, for example, Wykstra 1984). Having provided a broad context for the problem of evil, I return, in the next subsection, to African philosophers' engagement with the problem.

---

[7] The idea of the significant exercise of free will should not be confused with Sterba's notion of significant freedom. Unlike Sterba, Swinburne does not step into the domain of political philosophy.

2.4 Limited God Theism and Evil in the World

What will probably strike the African reader about the previous section is the centrality of the concept of freedom to Western theodicies. The importance of freedom is captured by Plantinga when he notes that: 'A world containing creatures who are significantly *free* (and *freely perform* more good than evil actions) is more valuable, all else being equal, than a world containing no free creatures at all' (Plantinga 1977, 30). The preoccupation with freedom is markedly absent in the thought of African philosophers of religion. Even when a theistic philosopher like Gyekye appeals to free will, he does not vigorously follow this line of thought. Instead of freedom, limited God theists like Wiredu, the Chimakonams, Bewaji, and Fayemi focus on responsibility and harmony in their characterisation of the relation between the limited God and the world.

2.4.1 Wiredu on God, Omnipotence, and Evil

Wiredu thinks that it is more plausible to assume that evil exists in the world because God is limited than to invoke the subtleties of the free will defence to show why a perfect God allows evil in the world. He observes that in traditional Akan thought, 'God himself comes to be thought of as the model of a father who has laid well-intentioned plans for his children which are, however, sometimes impeded not only by their refractory wills but also by the grossness of the raw materials he has to work with' (Wiredu 1998, 41). He makes three salient points, namely: (1) Humans have the ability to act responsibly or irresponsibly. (2) God is a limited entity. (3) Evil is a necessary part of the furniture of the world.

While Wiredu accepts that human beings have the ability to act responsibly, he denies that free will is a basic feature of the human being that is either exercised or not exercised, at least in the context of Akan thought. He instructively equates free will with responsibility. He asserts that: 'An individual is responsible (or free) if and only if she is amenable in both thought and action to rational persuasion and moral correction' (Wiredu 1996, 130). He does not see any fundamental opposition between free will and determinism. He is persuaded that determinism is true. For Wiredu, even the choices that humans make, with reason as a dependable guide, are conditioned by psychological motives and ethical considerations. He appeals to the African conception of the person to shed light on the idea that to act freely is to act responsibly. Normative African personhood regards the individual basically as a social self that acquires full personhood in degrees over a lifetime through internalising the moral norms of the society and becoming morally enhanced. In African moral tradition, the terms *human being* and *person* are not equivalent concepts. A human being is a biological entity in space and time while a person is a human being who has internalised the moral values of the society and acts in a responsible and humane manner. In this sense, the African notion of personhood is normative.

Freedom consists in the social being's exercise of their reason in making choices that have an ethical content recognisable to the society. Freedom is not understood in Plantinga's libertarian sense nor in Swinburne's sense of a great good whose significant employment outweighs all the evils in the world and the safeguarding of which morally justifies God allowing evil. Wiredu is less interested in theodicies and more interested in the preservation of social harmony, having understood evil as a necessary part of the structure of the world. Freedom is not in itself a great good, not the condition for moral behaviour, but, rather what we perceive in practice when we act in socially approved ways. The norms of the society guide social approval of individual actions. These norms, however, are always moral norms since they are formulated to promote human well-being.[8]

Since God is limited, he cannot compel human beings to always choose the right path. Indeed, God *created* the world, but only in the sense of a designer, according to Wiredu. He appears to think that attributing creatorship to God means granting God omnipotence. One can say that a carpenter designs a table but does not create it, going by Wiredu's logic. The carpenter produces something new using a material already at hand – that is, wood. While God's work of designing the world involves innovation which his great power and knowledge makes possible, he does not create ex nihilo. Like the carpenter, God produces the world from resources that are already at hand. Wiredu calls these resources gross matter. He implies, without arguing further, that the necessity of the occurrence of moral and physical evil is abstracted from the very nature of the gross matter.

Going by Wiredu's assertion, God is not the cause of evil, for he is good. He could not have predicted all the evils that would unfold in the world he was designing, in the beginning, because he is not omniscient. One might expect a God who creates from pre-existing materials to have a very good predictive power. Wiredu's God possesses such a good predictive power because he knows many, or most, things in advance. He does not have to know all things in advance to be considered a being with a very good predictive power. He cannot intervene in the course of nature to eliminate evil or prevent it because he is not omnipotent. For Wiredu, then, the reality of moral and physical evil does not require a theodicy. It rather indicates the tragic dimension of a deterministic

---

[8] Wiredu believes in the universality of the moral principle of sympathetic impartiality. This principle regulates interpersonal relationships and demands the harmonious union of justice and empathy. It is when impartial justice and empathy harmonise in human conduct that human well-being is guaranteed (Wiredu 1996, 31).

universe. In this deterministic universe, however, moral responsibility is a burden which human reason places on individuals.

2.4.2 The Harmony-God and Evil in the World

The Chimakonams are, perhaps, the African philosophers of religion who come closest to developing a theodicy. However, they defend a limited God view rather than traditional theism. As noted in Section 2.2, the harmony-God of the Chimakonams legitimises his existence by acting as the sustainer of harmony in the world. Cordeiro-Rodrigues and Chimakonam (2022) have suggested that if the harmony-God was a perfect God in possession of all the omni-properties, it would be easy to argue that he allows evil in the world in order to safeguard the greater good of harmony. But, then, the Chimakonams accept that God is limited. Yet he harmonises variables and relations in the world because he is sufficiently powerful and knowledgeable. He is not the cause of evil and cannot eliminate it. It sometimes appears that the harmony-God is all-powerful, such that he allows evil in the world to safeguard harmony. However, Jonathan O. Chimakonam understands harmony in terms of the quantitative and qualitative balance of diverse variables in the world rather than in terms of completeness or perfection.

In a work that Jonathan O. Chimakonam co-authored with Cordeiro-Rodrigues, one reads that the harmony-God is:

> [C]apable of rewarding and punishing, blessing and cursing as traits in his nature. He does evil not because of some good end but because it pleases Him to do so. In Him, there is a harmony of good and evil. His worshippers aim to always be in His good book. When they fall out with Him, they make sacrifices to appease Him. (Cordeiro- Rodrigues and Chimakonam 2023, 64)

This picture of the harmony-God indicates limitation. It is even implied that the harmony-God is capricious given that he inflicts evil on the entities he created because the conduct gives him satisfaction. This indicates a serious moral shortcoming in the harmony-God. While the Chimakonams suggest that God has an inherent tendency to do evil, like other entities, they do not state clearly how evil infects the world. They assume that the principle of evil is embedded in the structure of reality. Evil is, therefore, something necessary. There are a few issues that the idea of a harmony-God throws up.

It is not yet clear why the powerful harmony-God cannot do more than he does. It is not clear why there has to be a quantitative and qualitative balancing of good and evil instead of the reduction of evil, so that there is more good than evil in the world. One may point out that the harmony-God has been granted less responsibility than he ought to have in view of his great power and to the extent that he is not a malevolent being. While the Chimakonams submit that the harmony-God can do evil, they also acknowledge that he does good. He will be deemed a malevolent entity only if he is significantly or thoroughly evil. The fact that he does evil sometimes can be accounted for by his imperfection. He does not inflict evil because he is malevolent. The knowledge of the harmony-God must be proportional to his considerable power given that the balancing act requires great knowledge and skill. The magnitude of his power and knowledge and the fact that he is not malevolent require that there should be a good, perhaps morally justifiable, reason for the good–evil balancing act. The assertion that the harmony-God 'does evil not because of some good end but because it pleases Him to do so' leaves gaps in the idea of a limited God whose major task after creation is sustaining the balance of variables in the world (Cordeiro-Rodrigues and Chimakonam 2023, 64).

One may be tempted to regard the harmony-God as a capricious deity. But the very notion of harmony renders this interpretation of the harmony-God problematic. For a being to desire harmony and work to establish and sustain it, whims cannot be at play as motivating factors. Perhaps what the Chimakonams have not pondered yet is the idea that the good–evil balancing is necessary for the persistence of the world. Quantitative and qualitative imbalance would mean not simply instability but the eventual disappearance of the world since its emergence is motivated by the goal of harmony even as its sustenance is dependent on the actuality of harmony. If there is actual disharmony in the world, it means there is no harmony-God. If there is no harmony-God in the world the Chimakonams describe, there will be no world at all. This point is tentatively submitted here. A fuller exploration will be undertaken in the future.

2.4.3 Bewaji and Fayemi on the Limited God

Like Wiredu and the Chimakonams, Bewaji and Fayemi accept that God is not perfect. Unlike the Chimakonams, Bewaji and Fayemi stress the moral dimension of God. Bewaji's study of traditional Yoruba religious thought persuades him that what one may regard as evil perpetrated by God may be morally justifiable punishment for an action that contradicts divine law (Bewaji 1998, 10). God is indeed limited in power and knowledge to the extent that his power and knowledge are not of the order of omnipotence and omniscience. But he is still a very great being, the creator and sustainer of the world. His power is unrivalled in the world. If God is this great and he is on the whole a benevolent being that harms only breakers of his impartial law, why is there so much evil in the world? Granted, he cannot eliminate evil since he is not all-powerful. But it seems that he has sufficient powers to reduce the evil in the world on a scale far beyond human capacity. Bewaji appeals to moral relativism to calm his unease about not having given God more responsibility for the evil in the world that God created. According to Bewaji:

> [E]vil, as such, is not understandable. Nothing is intrinsically evil. We call something evil because it does not favor us or because it causes us distress. We may not know or understand the reason for the event or action … His attributes do not preclude the device and use of evil for the betterment of society. God is the creator. He created everything, both positive and negative. Why? We cannot know. His ways are incomprehensible. (Bewaji 1998, 11)

One moment Bewaji asserts that evil is not objectively grounded in reality, and the next moment he suggests that evil is real and God may bring about a good state through evil. The appeal to moral relativism is not strongly persuasive. Evil constitutes a harm that causes suffering for entities in the world. It is counter-intuitive to deny the objectivity of the report of sufferers in the world. Denying the objectivity of the report is tantamount to denying the reality of the sufferer. The God Bewaji describes is a very powerful being. Could he have done more to reduce the evil in the world? Bewaji's answer seems to be of this type: God is already doing his best by producing some good out of evil.

Fayemi notes that there are moral, physical, and spiritual evils in the world. Moral evil, broadly construed, arises from creatures' misuse of their free will while physical evil is harm caused by the structural organisation of the world. Spiritual evil refers to harm caused by supernatural forces like deities and spirits. He notes:

> One may argue that Olodumare can be exonerated from being responsible for some forms of evil: social and psychological evil, moral evil, and intellectual evil. These evils are man-made – products of human actions through freedom, choice, and responsibility. However, Olodumare and the coterie of divinities are blameworthy and cannot be rationally defended in the face of physical and spiritual evils. (Fayemi 2012, 12)

Like Wiredu, he concedes that God does not cause humans to do evil. However, God is the creator of the world and of the evilly inclined lesser deities that inflict harm on humans. Fayemi suggests that the limited God is powerful enough to prevent spiritual and physical evil. If God is worthy of blame for the reality of physical and spiritual evil, then he could have done better. Fayemi does not analyse the problem of limitation, creation, and moral responsibility, but he appears to believe that not only could God have done better, but he could have prevented physical and spiritual evil. In Section 2.6, I will argue that God could not have prevented physical and spiritual evil. In Section 3, I will argue that God being blameworthy, or morally responsible, consists chiefly in his creating an imperfect world with evil in it.

2.5 Limited God Non-theism and Evil in the World

Attoe best represents the non-theistic strand of the limited God view. Like Wiredu, he approaches the question of God's relation with the world from a materialistic perspective. The world is a rigidly determined space with God as its first cause. At first, the idea of a first cause gives the impression that Attoe is staking out a traditional theistic stance. But then he announces that the first cause is, in fact, only a mechanical principle and initial condition of the world. God is the initial condition that kick-started a chain of events that resulted in the unfolding of the world.[9] God is an *It* that lacks agency whatsoever. Attoe's God is so severely limited that he is unconscious, a completely impersonal principle that may, in fact, be understood in terms of its connection with a physical constant like energy. Attoe's choice of energy is influenced by his reading of the first law of thermodynamics, which states that energy cannot be created nor destroyed (Attoe 2022a, 30).

If God is an unconscious material entity, he cannot have any responsibility for the evil in the world, in Attoe's view. Should evil then be deemed to exist necessarily as part of the structure of a material universe? Attoe responds by adopting a more radical view. He revisits Bewaji's suggestion that nothing is intrinsically evil. According to Attoe:

> And so the idea that it is somehow the responsibility of God to mitigate evil, and that It either fails to do so or fails to exist, is a moot one. This new African vision of the supreme being does not include, as a property of God, conscious- ness or personality . . . And what really is evil? Evil is harm, and the concept of harm is an anthropocentric concept that simply reflects our understanding that a certain event, occurrence or encounter is not to our benefit or not to the benefit of those to whom we are empathetic. (Attoe 2022b, 23)

The relativist stance depends in part on the assumption that our evaluation of the evilness of a thing is subjective or anthropocentric. But, then, suffering is a measure of the evil in the world, and it is not only human beings that suffer. Animals clearly suffer, given their capacity for sentience, with the intensity of their suffering proportional to the extent of the actualisation of sentience. Thus a dog may be said to suffer more than a trichoplax. A number of African

---

[9] Attoe's claim that God is a mechanical first principle of the world does not appear to have been demonstrated. While he asserts that God is a first cause, he also notes that in the very beginning, God coexisted with other entities (Attoe 2022a, 2022b). It is the interaction between God and the primordial entities that caused the evolution of the world. If God always coexisted with other entities, he could not be a first cause. If he is indeed a first cause, Attoe has not demonstrated this.

philosophers and Western scholars who work on African philosophy have noted that traditional African ontology and ethics support not only anthropocentrism, but also biocentrism and ecocentrism (see, for example, Magesa 1997; Taringa 2006; Behrens 2010; Chuwa 2014; Ikuenobe 2014; Etieyibo 2017; Molefe 2018). While the African anthropocentric view privileges human beings and seems to set humans over against nature, the biocentric and ecocentric views grant animals, plants, and inanimate things moral status. This is the case because these entities possess vitality/vital force, the divine essence that God distributes throughout the world (see Etieyibo 2017; Molefe 2018; cf. Horsthemke 2017). The African biocentric view asserts that entities like animals have intrinsic value given that they share in the vitality/force that connects everything in the universe. Vital force is a measure of the life principle and has been equated with life by African philosophers like Molefe (2018) and Laurenti Magesa (1997). The higher the concentration of vitality, or life, in an entity, the more keenly it reacts to pain.

One way of accounting for cross-species application of the concept of suffering is regarding evil as something springing from an objective principle in the universe, a real capacity that different individuals and species identify as harm, an existential threat that manifests in diverse ways. In this sense, it can be argued that evil is a real phenomenon of the universe that brings about suffering. Whether the moral relativist agrees with this point of view or not, what is obvious is that the unconscious God Attoe describes cannot be blamed for the evil in the world. Attoe's stance may as well be atheistic, although he denies that he is proposing an atheological viewpoint.

2.6 Why the Logical and Evidential Problem Does Not Arise in African Philosophy of Religion

The problem of evil is one of the fundamental questions of Western philosophy, as Section 2.3 makes apparent. The status of this problem is not fundamental in African philosophy. The problem does arise in the thought of theistic African philosophers like Gyekye and Oduwole. However, African theistic philosophers have not rigorously engaged the problem. For the limited God proponents, the problem of evil is either a moot point or a muted one. The logical and evidential problem of evil is a moot point to the extent that it can be asserted that the concept of limitation perfectly explains why God permits evil in the world. This view is held by philosophers like Wiredu, Bewaji, Oladele Balogun (2009), the Chimakonams, and Attoe. The logical and evidential problem of evil is a muted point to the extent that the concept of limitation allows God to be a creator with the acknowledgement of the (moral) responsibility that goes with the title of creator. This view is held by philosophers like Agada, Fayemi, and Cordeiro-Rodrigues. This view submits that while it is true that the concept of limitation indicates degrees of incapacity, one must not understand the concept in an absolutist sense.

An absolutist sense of limitation presents God as an utterly powerless entity. Yet the description of God that one finds in much of the limited God literature presents the deity as a powerful and knowledgeable creator. The limitation of God is in the context of the applicability of the notions of omnipotence, omniscience, and omnibenevolence. Attoe is perhaps the only African philosopher who can legitimately espouse an absolutist understanding of limitation since he conceives God as completely lacking agency. Philosophers who think that the problem of evil is only muted in African philosophy believe that the limited God may have more responsibility than has been granted to him (see Fayemi 2012; Agada 2023a). God is, after all, a creator and could have refrained from creating an imperfect world. If he could create a world, he must have been knowledgeable enough to have foreseen many or some of the evils that would emerge in the created world.

The limited God cannot prevent the occurrence of evil in the world and could not have done a better job of creation. He reached his maximum creative capacity while creating the world which, accordingly, is the best possible world that a limited God could create. He cannot prevent or eliminate evil in the world because evil is a necessary component of the world. The material he employed at creation hour already contained the germs of evil. Indeed, God himself already contained in himself the germs of evil. Hence, some limited God proponents assert that God can do evil, at least sometimes.[10] The most that a limited God can do is reduce or ameliorate evil after it has occurred.

Thus the concept of limitation conclusively explains God's inability to make the world better overall, his failure to create a better world than our actual world at creation hour. The Chimakonams can respond to the claim that the harmony-God can do better by pointing out his deficiency in the aspect of goodness. Since the harmony-God is limited in goodness, a moral outcome is not always his target. He may perpetrate evil just to please himself, consistent with his limitation in goodness. A legitimate criticism that arises unavoidably is whether there is truly a harmonious balance of good and evil in the world. A detailed discussion of this matter is, however, beyond the scope of this section.

Nevertheless, there is a sense in which the limited God can be said to be blameworthy and morally responsible for the evil in the world even though evil

---

[10] Interestingly, the God of the Old Testament also does evil, at least sometimes. In Exodus 32:14 one reads: 'And the LORD repented of the evil which he thought to do unto his people' (King James Version).

exists necessarily. God being morally responsible does not mean that he could have made the world better. Rather, it indicates that God should have refrained from creating the world. He will be absolved of moral responsibility if it can be shown that an inherent necessity in God's nature compels him to create an imperfect world against his own better judgement. That is, the limited God cannot help but create. To the best of my knowledge, no limited God proponent has argued convincingly that the limited God is under such necessity. I will revisit this theme in Section 3. This section will engage the problem of limitation and evil from the perspective of the philosophy of consolationism. In Section 3, I will develop the *mood* perspective of God and present it as a unique contribution to African and global philosophy of religion.

2.7 Conclusion

In this section, I explored the problem of evil in relation to the existence of the limited God and argued that the logical and evidential problem of evil does not arise in the context of the limitation thesis. The limited God cannot eliminate evil. Nevertheless, I pointed out that there is a sense in which the limited God, who is not the cause of evil, is morally responsible for the evil in the world, for the reason that he did not refrain from creating a world that he knew would be marred by evil from the beginning. In the next section, I will explore this matter and determine whether it can truly be said of God that he cannot help creating an imperfect world. It should be noted at this juncture that one cannot invoke ignorance to account for why the limited God creates a world with plenty of evils in it. This stance is only applicable to Attoe's religious thought for obvious reasons.

3 The Limited God, Creation, and Moral Responsibility

3.1 Introduction

In the previous sections, I focused on the broad articulation of the limited God thesis with direct reference to the various stances of a number of leading African philosophers of religion. For proper context, I compared the limitation thesis with the African perfect God thesis in Section 1. In Section 2, I critically highlighted the limitation stances of philosophers like Kwasi Wiredu, Jonathan O. Chimakonam, Aribiah D. Attoe, Ademola K. Fayemi, and John Ayotunde I. Bewaji in relation to the logical and evidential problem of evil. In this section, I deepen the exploration of the capacity of the limited God with special focus on the consolationist standpoint.

While previous sections pay particular attention to the literature, this section will condense my own original contribution to the literature. I again revisit the question of the extent of the incapacity of the limited God with regard to the reality of evil in the world. I delineate the scope of the powers of the limited God who creates the world in search of consolation and raise the question of whether one can argue for an inherent necessity in the rational and emotional constitution of the consolation-seeking and consolation-giving God that compels him to create a world with evil even when he has sufficient knowledge to predict from the beginning the future course of the imperfect world he is creating for self-consolation. Within the framework of the consolationist system of speculative metaphysics, I raise and explore the questions of God's passibility and the desirability of non-existence from the human standpoint. I argue that whether the limited God of consolation philosophy is conceived as being conditioned by *mood* to create imperfect worlds such as ours in the pursuit of self-consolation or he is conceived as freely creating an imperfect world, again in the pursuit of self-consolation, this God has a moral responsibility to ameliorate the evils in the world by reason of his possession of the considerable powers and knowledge required for world-creation and for not refraining from world-creation. I assert that the limited consolation God does not have to be omnipotent and omnibenevolent to seek to ameliorate the suffering in the world. In this section, I will often use the terms *universe* and *world* to indicate the totality of reality that exists eternally and a defined space created by God from materials available in the eternal universe, respectively. In this sense, the universe is an immense, formless totality while the world is a well-defined space and a product of divine creativity.

The reader will be tempted to raise the question of the existence of the limited consolation God. This is a legitimate question. However, a philosophical defence of the existence of the limited consolation God is beyond the scope of this Element. My task consists of exploring the emergent question of the relation between the limited God and a world that reveals evidence of evil and the extent to which the limited God, if he exists, is morally responsible for the suffering of creatures.

3.2 The Limited God in Consolationist Metaphysics

In this section, I provide a more detailed explanation of the concept of *mood* and unpack it in a concise manner that facilitates the demonstration of the objectives of the section. I have extensively discussed the concept of *mood* in other works (see Agada 2015, 2019, 2020a, 2023a). I will provide a clear summary in this section and connect the doctrine of *mood* to the concept of consolation before discussing the attributes of the limited God of consolation.

3.2.1 On the Idea of Mood

A number of African metaphysical thinkers have attempted to understand Afro-relationality in terms of a basic property that all entities participate in. Afro-relationality entails Afro-communitarianism. Afro-relationality is the view that entities in the universe are interconnected and interdependent, whether entities and phenomena are conceived in physicalist or non-physicalist terms. The Afro-relational view is widely accepted in the literature (see, for example, Tempels 1959; Mbiti 1969; Gbadegesin 1991; Gyekye 1995; Tutu 1999; Bujo 2001; Menkiti 2004; Teffo 2004; Nkondo 2007; Abraham 2010; Dzobo 2010; Oyowe and Yurkivska 2014; Ebo 2022). Placide Tempels (1959) proposes that the basic stuff that is shared by all things is vital force. For Kwame Gyekye (1995), the fundamental principle is *sunsum*. For Socrates Ebo (2022), the fundamental principle is *matser*, something that is neither basically matter nor mind-stuff but which expresses itself in material and non-material dimensions. Tempels and Gyekye conceive the fundamental animating principle as an immaterial principle distributed by an omnipotent and omniscient God. A difficult problem that Tempels and Gyekye encounter, which I seek to overcome with the idea of *mood*, is explaining the interaction between material objects and the immaterial, or spiritual, fundamental principles that they posit as the basis of interconnection and interdependence. To unify the African universe of material and immaterial entities, I propose that *mood* is the basic animating principle of the universe. Unlike Gyekye and Tempels, I regard the fundamental animating principle as an event constituted by the dynamic of mind–matter unity. *Mood* is an event in the sense that it has no fixed mind–matter border, as what seems to be a demarcating border is constantly transgressed. The transgression of borders means that a mind quality can present aspects of a material quality even as a material quality can exhibit characteristics of mentality. Thus a human being, for example, can be constituted by material and experiential or immaterial properties.

The dynamism of *mood* is made possible by its inherent yearning essence. The transgression of borders indicates the goal of becoming which is yet never fully achieved since whatever is defined in terms of yearning is fundamentally incomplete. Yearning is the quest of a thing to become either something else or to surpass its current condition by modifying itself in relation to other entities. Given that *mood* is the prototype of mentality and materiality, the evolution of which produces material and non-material objects, I define *mood* as a proto-mind (2015, 2019, 2020b, 2022b). The term *mind* in *proto-mind* does not indicate the immateriality of *mood* but rather indicates the dynamism or flux state of *mood*. Elsewhere I noted that:

> Mood is the most fundamental essence or feature of reality. This means that it *is*, such that existence cannot be conceived without it. It is what is most real,

present everywhere and in all beings, directing conscious and unconscious behaviour in animate and inanimate things. According to this hypothesis, and I present it as a metaphysical speculation rather than scientific certainty, the building block of things is an event in which materiality and immateriality are implicated as moments of this fundamental reality. *Mood* is thus a prototype of body as well as mind. The mental and the bodily coexist in this essence as moments of reality that continually transgress their borders to constitute a dynamic unity. (Agada 2022b, 67)

Given that *mood* expresses itself as incompleteness and in view of the fact that it animates the universe, the consolationist universe is an eternal universe in a state of perpetual becoming. *Mood* continually strives towards the goal of completeness but never attains it. Accordingly, the universe of *mood* is eternal. With *mood* posited as the fundamental animating principle and the prototype of material and immaterial objects and qualities, the primordial mind–matter event, it becomes clearer how a universe of material and immaterial phenomena can exist. It becomes easy to make sense of Afro-relationality since both material and immaterial phenomena exhibit the yearning essence of *mood* which underlies them. A material thing has the essence of yearning just as an immaterial thing has the essence of yearning. Both the material thing and the immaterial thing are expressions of *mood*. They are able to interact and constitute entities because they have the same essence. Thus everything in the universe can attract every other thing and interconnect with it. The assessment of the success or failure of the idea of *mood* in accounting for mind–matter interaction is beyond the scope of this section (see Agada 2019 and 2023b for a deeper exploration of the mind–body problem).

From the foregoing, it is obvious that the universe of *mood* is a universe of yearning, where entities are in a state of perpetual becoming. From the human epistemological standpoint, completeness is indicated as the reason for the endless activity of change even as this goal is unrealisable since the nature of yearning is to seek to *become* in perpetuity. Accordingly, the universe of *mood* is an incomplete and imperfect universe. Any entity constituted by *mood* necessarily is incomplete. That which is incomplete is imperfect.[11] Since *mood* is ubiquitous in the universe, nothing escapes imperfection. What kinds of entities are constituted by *mood*? Examples encompass all actual and possible entities in the universe of *mood*. We can mention God, deities, human beings, animals, and mountains as entities

---

[11] The philosopher Innocent I. Asouzu (2007) has argued that while incompleteness characterises individual things, sharing and interaction increasingly complete individuals. Asouzu's stance on the matter is more optimistic than my own to the extent that in consolation philosophy, completeness is impossible. While Asouzu considers the world as a place for the realisation of human joy through having communal relations, consolation philosophy regards the world as a tragic manifestation of *mood*.

constituted by *mood*. We can also mention entities that are yet to exist – for example, the unborn and currently undiscovered entities and phenomena. A universe constituted by *mood* and which strives after an impossible completion or perfection is a tragic universe. Its very existence is consolatory in the sense that it is all that could have been, or the best possible universe. A best possible universe marred by evil is given as a consolation, a compensation for the impossibility of a *best* universe. In the absence of the best state of existence, what is actual or available is a better state of existence in relation to the worst or a worse state and is therefore consolatory. In a later section, I will raise the question of whether a consolatory world created by a limited God who seeks and gives consolation, a world with plenty of suffering and seemingly gratuitous evil, is better than a nil world or a non-existent world. In a universe of *mood*, moments of meaning available to conscious entities like human beings are consolations. These consolations make life more meaningful, but they do not change the fact that a universe of *mood* is, in the first place, a tragic universe that exists eternally in search of the impossible state of completeness.

3.2.2 On the Category of Consolation

I noted in Section 3.2.1 that the universe of *mood* is a tragic one that necessarily unfolds imperfectly given the yearning essence of *mood* and the eternity of futile striving for the completeness indicated by the conscious and unconscious activity of entities. Yearning motivates activity that I speculate to be directed towards the completion of being, or *mood*, in the actualisation of a highest condition of existence. This highest condition will translate to a state of perfection of *mood*, the completeness of the universe. To understand how a perfect universe will look, one can picture a world without moral and physical evil, one in which planetary and galactic systems work harmoniously or orderly to avoid wear and tear and support the being of sentient and conscious entities in the universe. In this complete universe, not only will conscious entities have the capacity to refrain from doing evil, harmful occurrences like earthquakes will not occur.

Human beings will have full knowledge of why the universe exists and their own purpose for existing in the first place. In a complete universe, humans will be able to live forever and be so constituted that boredom will not disrupt their perfect state of being. Indeed, a complete universe mirrors the Kingdom of God that the Bible describes in vivid detail, an indication that consolationist speculation is not strange to human thinking (see Agada 2019). One may wonder at this juncture how restless human beings can defeat the menace of ennui which some Western philosophers propose as a cogent reason for rejecting immortal existence (see, for example, Williams 1973; Schopenhauer 2000; Bortolotti and

Nagasawa 2009; Metz 2012a). Since my focus here is the African consolationist system, I will not explore the Western discourse on the boredom of immortal existence. Note that I define *mood* as a yearning essence. *Mood* attaining its goal of perfection will mean an end to striving and the beginning of a condition of perpetual satisfaction. Moody entities would have progressed to a state of being that has defeated the menace of boredom. Thus boredom would not afflict sentient beings existing forever in a complete universe.

However, to be a moody creature means to strive futilely towards the highest state of being that sustained conscious and unconscious activity indicates, in the framework of consolationist metaphysics. Human beings, the most intellectually advanced creatures in the known world, have no certain knowledge of why they and the universe exist. At most, they can only speculate about it, just as I speculate that perfection is the goal. This epistemic deficiency is fatal to any philosophical construction that asserts that human existence as a whole is meaningful. To lack the knowledge of the *why* means human existence is ultimately meaningless from the human standpoint.[12] The actual meanings that make up our joyful moments are mere consolations. Just as the universe of *mood* is consolatory, so are the joys of an ultimately incoherent existence of futile striving consolatory.

While discussing the concept of consolation, I observed elsewhere that:

> The term consolation is a category of the mind that condenses the fact of a monumental cosmic drama of tragic dimensions in which mentality and materiality tantalisingly suggest the idea that there is a directionality attached to this monumental drama, on the basis of which it is perhaps plausible to believe that human life has meaning and that the universe is rational, notwith-standing the absence of epistemic certainty about what kind of final purpose motivates the endless striving of nature ... Consolation encompasses the fact of the reality of joy in the sphere of human existence. (Agada 2022b, 63)

The term *mentality* indicates consciousness and the capacity for thinking that enables humans to judge the degree to which their lives are purposeful. The term *materiality* indicates that seemingly inanimate things express their yearnings in terms of activity that appears regulated by laws of nature. While a piece of rock itself is not conscious in the way that the human being is conscious, it has experience in the sense that it is active at the micro or subatomic level and one can imagine what it is like for the rock to be what it is (cf. Ofuasia 2022c, 276–277). With particular reference to the human being, the observer of the universe, yearning exhausts itself in activities that seek to increase joy and reduce sadness. But I argued earlier that the

---

[12] This stance contrasts with the stance of Aribiah D. Attoe (2023) who also holds a pessimistic view of human existence. However, while I emphasise the epistemic deficiency, Attoe empha-sises the tragic dimension of death.

universe in which the human being strives is a tragic universe. Consequently, the moments of joy that assure us that life is worth living are mere consolations.

3.2.3 The Limited God

In Section 1, I demonstrated the rootedness of two opposing conceptions of God in the African philosophy of religion literature, namely the perfect God and limited God views. My focus here is presenting the consolationist conception of the limited God, as already noted. In various works, I have sought to delineate the powers of the limited God, well aware that limitation does not equate impotence. In the consolationist framework, to say God is limited is the same as saying he lacks the omni-properties. Thus God is still powerful, knowledge-able, and benevolent. But the magnitude of these attributes is limited by the universal animating principle called *mood*, which constitutes God's essence just as it constitutes the nature of entities like human beings and animals. What makes the divine case exceptional is that God is a primordial being who is so knowledgeable about the workings of *mood* that he has mastered this principle; he becomes a creator through the manipulation of the resources of *mood* to produce the world. It is in this sense that God is called a creator. Accordingly, the God of consolation philosophy is conceived in a broad, theistic way even if not in the traditional theistic sense that makes God a perfect being.

I argued elsewhere (see Agada 2022b, 2023c) that God can be conceived of in three ways within the consolationist framework that provide a measure of the magnitude of his powers. First, one can conceive of God as an absolute first cause that brings time and space into existence and creates ex nihilo. Such a being would not only have always existed uncaused, but would wield powers so great that they would be measured in terms of omnipotence. This is the case since this God commands space and time into existence through the exercise of his will. Such a being can conceivably do everything logically possible. Such a being brings *mood* into existence. Second, one can conceive of God as a primordial being who emerges uncaused in an eternally existing formless universe animated by *mood* and manipulates *mood* to create a well-defined world considered as an expression of the divine power. This primordial being is uncaused in the sense of having emerged spontaneously in the *mood*-animated universe. That is, God simply began to exist. While the universe is the indes-tructible and unlimited totality that always was, a world is an appendage of the eternally existing universe that God creates in the exercise of his power and knowledge of the operation of *mood*, the universal animating principle. It is in this sense that the consolation God is a creator. Since *mood* is not an entity, there is no competition between it and God. While God is active and seeks to manipulate the principle that constitutes his nature and animates the universe, the principle itself is passive. While interrogating the concept of the consolation God through the conceptual lens of process thought, Emmanuel Ofuasia (2022c), has argued that the God I present is subordinate to *mood*, which he understands as the fundamental reality in consolationist metaphysics. I agree with Ofuasia when he asserts that *mood* limits the freedom of the consolation God but disagree with him when he places *mood* above God. *Mood* is a passive principle to the extent that it does not create even while containing in itself capacities for growth and development. God is an active entity that manipulates *mood* to spark the creative potentials latent in *mood*. God is the first being rather than *mood*. Drawing inspiration from Wiredu's distinction between universe and world, I will further show how God can be understood as a creator later in this section.

In the consolationist framework, God is not a perfect being because the universal animating principle that constitutes his nature is a limiting principle, as argued in Section 3.2.1. Note that *mood* is characterised by yearning and incompleteness. The God who emerges spontaneously as the maximal embodiment of *mood* is from the very beginning a being of yearning limited by what constitutes its nature. I presented this intuition in an early work and noted that: 'God . . . is not prior to *mood*, otherwise . . . God will have a nature not subject to yearning. He is not posterior to *mood*, otherwise He will be the God Wiredu describes as just somewhat higher in power and general excellence than an ancestor' (Agada 2023c, 570–571).[13]

I now come to the third way of conceiving of God. Here, God is regarded as subordinate or inferior to *mood* and as possessing powers only slightly greater than the powers of entities like ancestors and lesser deities. The God of the third way is severely limited. Okot p'Bitek (2011) must have this God in mind when he writes that: 'African peoples ... describe their deities as "strong" but not "omnipotent"; "wise", not "omniscient"; "old", not "eternal"; "great", not "omnipresent"' (2011, 42). The God of the third way is strong, wise, old, and great, but this is as far as his capacities go. This God is not far above ancestors and lacks the knowledge required to create or design worlds through the manipulation of the resources of *mood*. This God cannot sufficiently manipulate *mood*. It is just another entity in the universe of *mood*.

The God that consolation philosophy projects, the consolation God, is the God of the second way. The terms *strong*, *wise*, and *old* do not apply to him. While he is not omnipotent and omniscient, he is yet powerful, knowledgeable,

---

[13] This particular work was completed in 2018 but published late. At the time of its completion, my thought on *mood* was rapidly developing (see Agada 2023c). I now think that God is posterior to *mood* although he is not in competition with this principle.

and uncaused by any entity existing before him. He is powerful because he creates a world with a definite form from the resources of *mood* that are available to him in an eternally existing universe. He is knowledgeable because he understands what it takes to harness the resources of *mood* to create a world. He is uncaused by any entity existing before him in the sense that he is the first rational entity to emerge in a universe animated by *mood*. As already noted, the principle I identify as *mood* is not in competition with God because it is not an entity. What it does to God is limit him by reason of constituting God's nature and defining the deity as a yearning, incomplete entity in search of completeness. The consolation God desires omnipotence, omniscience, and omnibenevolence, but he has not achieved the state of perfection and cannot acquire the omni-properties given that *mood* constitutes his nature. This God exists as a consolation unto himself, for he seeks to be better but can only acquire the qualities of power, knowledge, and goodness on a magnitude that falls short of the omni-properties.

One can better appreciate the sense in which the consolation God is a creator by invoking Wiredu's implicit distinction between the universe as a totality and a world constructed by God using materials available in this universe. While there is ultimately one universe that has always existed, Wiredu concedes that God does create our actual world as an appendage of the universe. In the process of designing or constructing the world, new forms are brought into being. While arguing that the Akan reject the idea of creation out of nothing, Wiredu notes: 'If the "divine architect" fashioned the world out of some pre-existing raw material, then, however indeterminate it may have been, surely, somebody must have created it … obviously the notion of absolute nothingness will not make sense' (Wiredu 1998, 30).

Wiredu sets out to demonstrate that the idea of creation out of nothing is unintelligible within the traditional Akan conceptual framework. For him, the Akan God is properly a designer or architect rather than a creator. For Wiredu, the label 'creator' indicates a being who produces something entirely new out of nothing. Since God produces the actual world out of pre-existing materials, he does not initiate a process involving absolute novelty. Wiredu's insistence that God produces the world using a pre-existing material implies a distinction between our actual (known) world and a wider space of which God himself is a part and which contains a certain material that can be used for producing a world. Elsewhere, I identified this wider space as the universe, consisting of both the known reaches of space, our world, and the unknown reaches of space of which our world is a part (see Agada 2023a, 297). God and the pre-existing material exist in the universe. God, the new world he produces from the pre-existing material, this material itself, and the cosmic environment encompassing all these entities and phenomena constitute the totality called the universe. Wiredu analyses the Akan term for creator, *Oboade*, and points out a contradiction that supports his claim that the Akan God is a designer rather than a creator. *Oboade* indicates 'the maker of things. *Bo* means to make and *ade* means thing, but in Akan to *boade* is unambiguously instrumental; you only make something with something' (Wiredu 1998, 30). Yet it will appear that creativity goes into the production or making of a thing from available materials. For an entity to be called a creator, it does not have to produce something from absolute nothing. It is sufficient that the creator displays creativity in the production of something that previously was formless. Accordingly, Wiredu's God is a creator, like the consolation God. Like Wiredu's God, the consolation God creates from a pre-existing material and can be understood as a creator and not merely as a designer.

The consolation God exhibits creativity of immense proportions in producing a world from the resources of *mood* that animate the universe in which this God emerges as the most primordial being. In harnessing the resources of *mood* to create the world and all the sentient and non-sentient entities in this world, the consolation God displays great powers. Yet the definite world he creates is not perfect given his *mood*-limited nature. He desires creation and actually creates because he can create the best possible world. But the divine best was always going to be marred by the fundamental incompleteness of whatever *mood* undergirds. In exploring and mastering the secrets of *mood* to reach knowledge of the precise ways to manipulate the animating principle to create the world, God exhibits great knowledge. This knowledge is not of the order of omniscience, otherwise God would have gained knowledge of what it takes to create a world without moral and physical evil. Given the magnitude of knowledge he displays at the time of creation, he foresees from the beginning that the world he is creating will carry the imprint of *mood*, which is imperfection. He creates anyway because he is not omnibenevolent. While he is good and seeks to create a good world, his need to complete himself in the exercise of his powers and find greater consolation displaces his concern for the creatures he brings into existence in an incomplete world. While the consolation God might not have foreseen all the evils that would occur in his created world down to their minutest details, he was sufficiently knowledgeable to have foreseen most evils. Thus God has some moral responsibility for the world he creates. It is not necessary for him, at the time of creation, to have complete knowledge of all the evils that will occur, for him to accept responsibility for the evil that he does not cause but which he wilfully allows to proliferate. For God to be morally responsible, it is sufficient for him to be aware that the world he wants to create will be marred by evil and still go on to create when it is in his power to refrain from creating.

3.3 Creation, Evil, and the Limited God's Moral Responsibility

African philosophers of religion who embrace the limited God view have written much about limitation without saying much about what limits God. In this section, I pay attention to *mood* as the God-limiting principle. Still focused on the framework of consolationist metaphysics, I argue that if the power and knowledge of the limited God are such that he could have predicted the occurrence of all, or most, evils at the time of creation, then he bears responsibility for the reality of evil in the world he created even if he is not the cause of evil. Even if it can be shown that the consolation God could not have predicted the occurrence of some evils, he would still bear moral responsibility for ever accomplishing the task of creation, knowing from the very beginning that the world he would create out of the resources of *mood* would be marred by the imperfection of moral and physical evil. I remind the reader that God himself is always aware of his own limitation and cannot be excused on the basis of divine ignorance. I conclude the section with the exploration of the question of a necessity to create beyond the control of the consolation-seeking God that may absolve him of responsibility for moral and physical evil.

3.3.1 On Creation

While reflecting on Wiredu's thought on God's creatorship, I observed elsewhere that:

> If we can talk about the world as the creation of an author, then God is not a part of this world, but if we expand the world-space to include the universe (regarded as a totality of all existent things), then God becomes a part of the universe and also becomes subject to law-like conditions. (Agada 2023a, 297)

I further observed that:

> Wiredu appears to be using the term 'world' in the sense of Planet Earth and the known reaches of space. The terms 'world' and 'universe' are often used interchangeably to mean an immense totality of existing and potentially existent things . . . If God created the world, he must have done so from a pre-existing physical material (which Wiredu does not identify) in the universe and is, therefore, limited by this pre-existing stuff. (Agada 2023a, 297)

The distinction between world and universe (see Section 3.2.3) enables me to identify an existential space which God creates and which does not limit him, and a universe which exists eternally and which limits God, being animated by *mood* from the beginning. Thus the world God gives definite form to through creation is a direct expression of his imperfect nature. God stands apart from this world because before he created the world, it was only an idea in the divine mind. He creates the world and is different from it in the way that a poet who creates a poem using tools like ink and pen that predate the poem is different from the poem. Just as the poet stands in a relation of creator to his or her poem, so does God stand in a relation of creator to the world. Expectedly, he is not a creator in the traditional theistic sense. While he is apart from the world, he understands the suffering and pains that plague the world and can intervene in the world's affairs to reduce suffering to the best of his ability. A question that may stir in the mind of the reader at this point is the question of whether there is evidence that the limited God actually intervenes in the affairs of the world to reduce suffering. I will attend to this question in Section 3.5.

As part of the wider universe that is subject to the logic of *mood*, which is yearning, God becomes subject to this logic and is accordingly a limited being in search of perfection – that is, the omni-properties that he still lacks. The divine tragedy is the impossibility of the limited God attaining the omni-properties. This is also the tragedy of the world, for this limitation means that not only will created entities continue to contend with moral and physical evil (for a discussion of evil, see Section 2.2), but sentient and thinking beings like humans will be denied interaction with an omnipotent and omniscient being who can reveal to them the purpose of their existence and the purpose of the universe. This revelation would have enabled human beings to coherently evaluate their lives and factually decide that their lives are not ultimately meaningless in a mysterious universe. Additionally, the limited God attaining the omni-properties would create paradise-like conditions for creatures. If there is a good reason for the completed or perfected consolation God not to grant immortality to humans, he would at least eliminate most evils and only condone evils that contribute to the flourishing of human life within the span allotted to humans. This God would also let human beings know his reason for denying them immortality, and it would be a good reason.

A perfect God will be able to both predict the future occurrence of all evils at the time of creation and eliminate all or most evils. He will only permit some evils if these evils contribute to the flourishing of life. The consolation God I have been describing is able to predict the occurrence of most evils at the time of creation although he is unable to eliminate all or most of these evils. Note that this God is not powerful and knowledgeable like Wiredu's God, whose abilities in some respects are not much greater than the abilities of ancestors. For example, God's goodness is of the order of ancestral goodness (Wiredu 2010, 195). Ancestors are dead members of the community who have acquired great supernatural powers, are custodians of morality, and act as mediators between God and the living (see, for example, Cordeiro-Rodrigues and Agada 2022). The consolation God is considerably more powerful.

If the consolation God is knowledgeable enough to unlock the secrets of *mood* and create a world, he possesses the knowledge that facilitates an adequate prediction of the future course of the created world. Note that the consolation God fully understands the necessary existence of evil. He is aware that the conditions of the blossoming of moral and physical evil inhere in *mood* and that the act of creation will provide an opportunity for the evil principle in *mood* to proliferate beyond existing primordial spaces. Thus, even if one argues that the limited God creates on account of an inherent necessity that he cannot completely control or regulate, he always possesses sufficient knowledge of the consequences of his creative impulse. Moreover, having created the world, he has enough power to intervene in the affairs of the world and mitigate some evils, at the minimum.

3.3.2 The Limited God's Moral Responsibility

The notion of moral responsibility is not an easy one to articulate. Philosophers hold conflicting views about moral responsibility. In the Western tradition, which emphasises free will, determinism and compatibilism are factored into accounts of moral responsibility. In the African tradition, free will plays a less significant role in determining the coherence of an account of moral responsibility. Here, the emphasis is on knowledge and, by extension, the connection between personal conduct and communal well-being. In the Afro-communitarian literature, a person is a responsible human being who is able to resist the many conditioning states of affairs in the world and attain a socially commendable level of moral maturity (see, for example, Mbiti 1969; Menkiti 1984; Kaphagawani 2004; Eze 2008; Famakinwa 2010; Agada and Egbai 2018; Majeed 2018). This moral maturity includes taking responsibility for one's actions as a direct consequence of one possessing knowledge of right and wrong.

Accordingly, the idea of freedom is not decisive in the attribution of moral responsibility. In the African communitarian framework, morality is inextricable from the human person who comes into the world equipped with intellectual, social, and emotional capacities that make them able to learn and adjust to conditioning states of affairs. In this framework, a mentally ill individual cannot be held responsible for invading an orchard and harvesting ripe orange fruits. They are not responsible for their action because they lack sufficient knowledge of right and wrong. Wiredu provides perhaps the most interesting articulation of this view of moral responsibility when he proposes the equivalence of free will and responsibility. His seemingly compatibilist stance asserts that: 'An individual is responsible (*or free*) if and only if she is amenable in both thought and action to rational persuasion and moral correction' (Wiredu 1996, 130. Italics are mine.). A compatibilist stance typically asserts that free will and determinism are compatible. In the Afro-communitarian context, to be free is to act responsibly based on knowledge of what is right and what is wrong. The standard for measuring rightness and wrongness is established by the community through experiences that have been accumulated in the course of interpersonal relationships. A hungry man with a sane mind who invades his neighbour's orchard in the dead of night to harvest ripe orange fruits is indeed conditioned by hunger but remains responsible for his action given his prior knowledge of the wrongness of the action. He was aware that the society will receive his action with disapproval. The most he can expect from the society, the network of interpersonal relationships, is pity and leniency over the fact that hunger led him to steal oranges.

Peter F. Strawson in the Western tradition proposes a non-libertarian account of moral responsibility when he stresses the subjective dimension of the allocation of praise and blame. Praise and blame are to be understood in the context of interpersonal relationships, which involve the interplay of a range of reactive attitudes like anger, resentment, gratitude, etcetera (Strawson 1962, 5). We blame people from our own standpoint and deem them accountable if they deserve to be accountable. For him, responsibility attribution is less about someone's capacity to have acted differently in a given situation. Fernando Rudy-Hiller emphasises the epistemic aspect of responsibility attribution when he states the following four conditions required for responsibility attribution: (1) One must be aware of the meaning of one's actions. (2) One must be aware of the consequences of one's actions. (3) One must be aware of alternatives to one's actions. (4) There must be an absence of moral luck conditioning (Rudy-Hiller 2022, 56). The first three conditions are self-explanatory. Moral luck in the fourth condition refers to circumstances that see an actor allocated blame or praise with regard to an action and its consequences despite the actor not having complete control over the action being performed and the consequences. Moral luck introduces elements of unpredictability and incapacity. Moral luck happens when factors beyond the control of an actor influence the amount of praise or blame that the actor deserves.

From the foregoing, it can be argued that the limited consolation God has moral responsibility for exercising his creative impulse. The limited God's knowledge at the time he created the world *ex materia* encompassed awareness of the act of creation, the consequences of creation, and the alternative to creation, which is refraining from creating a world he knows will be marred by moral and physical evil given his own struggle for perfection. Perhaps an analogy of the dilemma of the man with AS genotype will shed more light on the consolation God's moral responsibility. Mr Oloture is a young man with AS genotype who falls in love with Miss Olofu who is also AS. Oloture has no ability to cure sickle-cell anaemia. He is well aware that marrying Olofu and having children will guarantee that at least one out of two or more children will be SS. While he cannot cure sickle-cell anaemia, it is in his power to prevent one more human being from experiencing the suffering that accompanies sickle-cell anaemia. He goes ahead to marry Olofu because he is deeply in love and cannot help himself. Oloture pleads the necessity of love when one of his children turns out to be SS and he is blamed for his child's suffering. Oloture is blameworthy because he always had sufficient knowledge of the consequences of marrying an AS woman and should have refrained from marrying Olofu. It does not matter that his action was conditioned by love impulses. The necessity involved in the love conditioning was never absolute before he got married. Any inferred rigid determinism follows the deed and is a subjective imposition on nature.

By extension, it does not matter that the consolation God could have been conditioned by the impulses of yearning that he contends with. Before the act of creation, the conditioning was never absolute. He creates to experience the emotion of satisfaction in the exercise of his considerable power, in his overall striving to more fully actualise himself. The consolation God reveals his limitation in goodness by not refraining from creating the world when it is in his power to refrain. Appeal to moral luck conditioning does not succeed here because what is of concern is not God creating the world and not being able to control certain consequences of creation, but God not refraining from creating the world with his knowledge of future deleterious consequences of creation. Not being omnibenevolent, he considers his own interest above the interest of the beings that will populate the world. He predicts the future course of the world, and suffers in advance over the future occurrence of suffering in the world (since he is good), but creates anyway because he has to console himself by exercising his creative powers. The consolation God putting his interest first is consistent with his limitation in goodness. Appeal to his limitation in goodness makes a stronger case for why he creates at all than appeal to determinism in a universe where *mood* (yearning) conditions all things. A universe of yearnings does not concede the operation of an absolute or rigid necessity since yearning means the possibility of novelty. A universe of yearning, the sort described by consolation metaphysics, is more tragic than determined since it is a universe where consolation compensates poorly for the impossibility of perfection. An action or event is only conditioned to the extent that yearning impulses influence the trajectory of the action or event in various degrees. In the context of the doctrine of *mood*, determinism is to be understood in terms of the inevitability of events and actions – that is, their necessary occurrence, the fact that they actually happen, and not the fact that the happening is rigidly conditioned at every point by antecedent factors that ensure a straight trajectory from the beginning to the terminus.

3.4 On the Consolation God's Passibility

It is obvious by now that the consolation God is passible. In the consolationist framework, God is the eternal mood of melancholy (see Section 1.6). I use the term *melancholy* to describe the experience of the emotions of joy and sadness in a world with a tragic dimension (Agada 2015, chapters 3 and 11). The *melancholy* aspect of joy and sadness reflects the futility of yearning. Yearning can be expressed as either a joy state or a sadness state depending on what motivates it in the field of experience. I have already noted that *mood* constitutes God's nature. God is capable of enjoying joy states and suffering sadness states. Since he is the primordial being who emerges spontaneously and will persist eternally, he is the eternal mood of melancholy. The term *melancholy* is a technical term in consolation philosophy that should not be confused with the medical term *melancholia*, which references a psychopathological condition, a depressive disorder (see Parker 2013). *Melancholy*, as I employ the term, simply indicates the tragic dimension of the incomplete universe and the condition of sentient beings that yearn all through the duration of their persistence, a yearning immediately recognisable as joy and sadness. A being is said to be melancholy if this being contends with the feelings of joy and sadness in an imperfect world where existence itself is given as a consolation. The term *melancholy* captures the creature's experience of hopefulness and hopelessness, meaningfulness and meaninglessness.

Divine impassibility is the view that God does not suffer or experience pleasure as a result of the actions of created entities like human beings. The doctrine of divine impassibility often goes together with the idea of divine aseity, the view that God is self-dependent and not affected by external conditions and entities (Chow 2018). Western theologians who accept traditional theism defend God's impassibility as a strategy that enables them to evade the conclusion that God is a limited entity (Kopel et al. 2022). The thinking of perfect-God theologians and philosophers of religion is that admitting that God suffers as a result of the suffering of humanity will mean that God does not possess the omni-properties and is in some sense deserving of pity. Divine passibility is the view that God is capable of suffering. He can only be indifferent to the suffering of his creatures if he is not a loving God. Christianity presents God as a loving deity. In recent years, the idea of divine passibility has been enlarged to include the belief that God has emotions (Scrutton 2013). In Western thought, process thinkers and proponents of open theism, for example, endorse divine passibility. Process thinkers inspired by the thought of Alfred North Whitehead, in fact, hold what one may call a limited God view (see Chow 2018). Open theism agrees with core traditional theistic views of God while conceding that God has emotions and relates intimately with human beings (Pinnock et al. 1994). Theologians and philosophers like Charles Hartshorne (1948), John Macquarrie (1978), and Jürgen Moltmann (1993) have argued that a God who does not share in human suffering is insensitive and incapable of love. African philosophers of religion have not paid close attention to the matter of God having emotions and sharing in human suffering. It is noteworthy that ATR conceives God as a remote deity (see, for example, Idowu 1973; Mbiti 1975; Ukpong 1983). God is believed to be too important to concern himself with details of human life. He is approached through inter-mediaries like the lesser deities and ancestors. Going by this understanding of God, one may conclude that God is somewhat indifferent to human suffering and has no emotions, at least in the way humans understand emotions. The harmony-God, for example, is more concerned about maintaining the good–evil balance in the world than reducing the amount of suffering in the world (see Section 2.3.2). He is not an emotional being. According to Jonathan O. Chimakonam and Amara E. Chimakonam:

> He [the harmony-God] brings the rain, but also brings the sun. He raises a forest only to blaze it down with fire. He gives a child to a mother and takes it the next day. He creates and destroys not just for the fun of it but for the overarching need to maintain the balance of good and evil. (2023, 334)

While the harmony-God is capable of doing good, he appears indifferent to human suffering and to the suffering of animals. In the framework of the limited God view, the divine lack of emotion or the indifference to suffering can be attributed to divine limitation in the dimension of goodness. If doing some bad things can be motivated by emotion, then the harmony-God may have emotions after all, even if he always seeks to achieve a cosmic balancing act at the expense of creatures. Going by Bewaji's account of God's quest for immortality as detailed in the Yoruba Ifa Corpus, it is obvious that the limited God has emotions. According to Bewaji (1998, 9), God became anxious about his status, whether he is mortal or immortal, and went around asking 'Wise men' questions concerning his immortality, after which he was assured of his immortality.

The God of consolation is passible and has emotions. This assertion follows logically from the claim that *mood* animates the universe and expresses itself as yearning. This yearning manifests in emotional and intellectual behaviour in entities like human beings. An example of emotional behaviour is the joyful response to good fortune while an example of intellectual behaviour can be working hard as a scientist to find cures for several types of cancer with the goal of advancing one's career and earning fame. The consolation God is not Attoe's impersonal principle but a personal deity. He is a being of power and knowledge because he understands the secret or workings of *mood* better than any other entity and to a very large degree, such that he achieves knowledge of what is required to produce new forms out of *mood*. The divine creative impulse expresses the divine yearning for perfection, the desire to attain the omni-properties, as I have already noted. In the process of creating a world *ex materia*, God populates expanded spaces with entities and derives satisfaction from the exercise of his powers. Some creatures that God creates – for example, human beings – honour God with worship. This worship involves a human–divine relation of dependence. Hence African scholars widely acknowledge that the African universe is a relational type. A God who derives consolation from creating worshipping creatures is a passible God. Attoe has observed that humans exist to legitimise God's existence. Attoe uses the term *legitimisation* in connection with the recognition and acknowledgement of a thing's existence. Solitary existence is devoid of legitimisation. He writes:

> Legitimisation, for me, is an ontological recognition that a thing is an existent thing. A flying unicorn is not a legitimised being since there is no ontological recognition of its being a thing in the world. The legitimisation of the existence of a flying unicorn would involve that unicorn's relationship with other beings and/or a recognition of that relationship by the being with which the flying unicorn has a relationship. (Attoe 2022c, 88)

Applied to the consolation God, legitimisation implies a desire for company and a loathing of solitude. A being that requires recognition and acknowledgement in the form of worship from creatures it created has emotions and understands the suffering of creatures and shares in the suffering, more or less. The consolation God shares in the suffering of creatures because he created them and understands their struggles with evil given that he also struggles to overcome the evil impulses inherent in *mood*. As a vastly powerful being, he substantially overcomes these impulses where human beings fail. But since the consolation God is not omnibe-nevolent, his own limitation and self-interest interfere with his empathetic cap-acity. He does the most he can to make the world better either through direct involvement (as in enhancing positive features of the world at the time of creation) or through human moral agency (by way of motivating humans who believe in him to do good in his name). As already asserted, God's self-interest motivated him to create the world even when he had adequate knowledge of the consequences of creation for creatures. He created anyway because of his need for legitimisation. At this juncture, one may wonder if the consolation God changes. The reply is in the affirmative. The consolation God, as a being of yearning, continues to grow in power, knowledge, and goodness. Given that he comes into existence spontaneously in an eternally existing universe, he will continue to exist. The question of his going out of existence will only arise if he attains his goal of becoming a being with the omni-properties. This will mark the apotheosis of his consolation. But, then, it seems reasonable to assume that a being that attains perfection will exist eternally and can no longer experience moments of diminution of power, knowledge, and goodness. The consolation God becomes the perfect God of traditional theism. The tragedy of the universe consists in the impossibility of the consolation God attaining the omni-properties. The system of consolationist metaphysics proposes that the divine quest will go on forever. Accordingly, this primordial being will exist forever.

3.5 Objections and Replies

I have only demonstrated God's causal responsibility, but not his moral responsibility.

It may be objected that the consolation God is not morally responsible for the evil in the world if he creates the world necessarily, and this seems the case since he is conditioned by *mood* to create an imperfect world. The consolation God is only causally responsible for the world, as Luis Cordeiro-Rodrigues (2023) argues. According to Cordeiro-Rodrigues, while it is obvious that the consolation God is causally responsible for the evil in the world as creator, it is not obvious that he is morally responsible for evil. The necessity, it may be argued, arises from God's conditioning by *mood*, which compels him to create. The point is that the divine yearning for consolation involves a deterministic process that necessitates the work of creation. I respond that the consolationist universe is not rigidly conditioned. While entities indeed yearn and are so constituted that they cannot attain perfection, they yet actualise themselves in varying degrees in the process of striving towards the impossible goal. The consolationist universe is more tragic than determined. Indeed, one can say that tragedies are determined, but, in the consolationist perspective, events are not rigidly conditioned. The tragedy I am referring to is the condition of a universe that exists as yearning. The heart of the matter is the circumscription of potentials which limitation imposes on yearning entities, rather than the question of rigid determinism. While the consolation God cannot attain the omni-properties, being limited by *mood*, he is capable of carrying out a range of actions in accordance with his status as a very powerful and knowledgeable being. For example, he can intervene in the affairs of the world to reduce some evils. God's moral responsibility follows from the possession of the knowledge required to determine the future trajectory of the world at the moment of its production or creation and the ability to have refrained from the creative exercise (see Section 3.3.2). The argument of necessity can hold only if God could not have refrained from creating a world that would be marred by evil. It is not necessary for God to be powerful and knowledgeable enough to eliminate or prevent most evils for him to be morally responsible. The limitation factor can be more effectively used to defend God's moral responsibility than his not having moral responsibility for the evil in the world. Being limited in goodness, he goes on to create the world in search of his own consolation at the expense of the consolation of the creatures he is bringing into existence (see Section 3.3.2).

To be is better than non-existence. A world with both good and evil is better than no world at all. Accordingly, the argument that God should have refrained from creating the world is weak.

Following from the first objection, it may be argued that God need not have refrained from creating the world because existence is better than non-existence. More precisely put, a world that contains both good and evil is better than a world that does not exist at all. Thus God creating a world with many evils side by side with many goods is not a bad thing for which he should be blamed. The evils that arise in the world are just necessary features of this world. Now, the bone of contention is not whether existence is better than non-existence per se. The heart of the matter is whether creating a world marred by evil is a morally acceptable thing to do. There is no doubt that there are many things in the world that provide human beings with pleasure. Yet the pleasure that accompanies the possession of goods like long life and rewarding jobs is more than diluted by the persistence of evils in the world. Some of these evils include everyday dangers that menace our lives at every moment and right in our homes – constant wars, the development of weapons of mass destruction, human malice, murder, greed, harmful sexual behaviour, hunger, natural disasters, incurable diseases, loneliness and boredom, and the many inconveniences of old age. Our lives add up to one long song of lamentation. To demand fortitude in the face of the constant pain that accompanies living is indeed a test of courage. Yet stoicism does not obscure the tragic dimension of life. The consolation God should have refrained from a creative exercise that he knows, *ab initio*, will cause the proliferation of entities and the multiplication of suffering. A no-world is better than a world marred by evil such as ours. In a no-world, human consciousness, the repository of pain and suffering, would not exist. This non-existence would mean that there would be no tormented consciousness in the world. The point I am making should not be confused with anti-natalism, although it rings pessimistic just like anti-natalism. Anti-natalism is the view that the living have an obligation not to bring people into the world in view of the harm they will be exposed to (see Benatar 2006; Metz 2012b; Singh

2012) or that bringing more people into the world disadvantages those already in the world by, for example, heightening the problem of population explosion (see Ehrlich 1968). My view goes deeper into the heart of the problem of existence by shifting responsibility for the major prevailing state of affairs (the creation of the world) to the consolation God.

God has a right to create the world as it is by reason of being the most powerful being in the world.

This objection assumes that might is right and that the consolation God is not good. If possessing power alone justifies God creating a world like ours, then he is not good. The consolation God would have a right to create a world marred by physical and moral evil if he was powerful enough to eliminate or prevent all or most evils and good enough to overlook his own interest and adequately consider the interest of creatures. Adequate consideration of the interest of creatures would mean that the consolation God allowing some evils in the would indicates that a divine plan to bring about a compensatory and/or better state that would compensate for the evils suffered in a lifetime, either in this world or in another world. This divine plan would nudge creatures towards the goal of perfection or bring about perfection outright. But a God who could accomplish these tasks would be an omnipotent, omniscient, and omnibenevolent being. The consolation God will have to be the God of traditional Christian theism and not the God whose conception in the consolationist perspective is inspired by ATR intuitions of divine limitation. Thus, while defending traditional Christian theism, Richard Swinburne (1998) asserts that (the perfect) God has a right to allow evil in the world since doing so is necessary for a greater good like freedom. Evil, in particular moral evil, becomes the price to pay to enjoy the good of freedom. In his words:

> Since one is obliged not to do that which one does not have the right to do and God always fulfils his obligations, the bad states which he allows to occur must be ones which he has the right to allow to occur ... many of the bad states which God allows to occur are ones which humans freely choose to inflict on each other ... bad states ... are the price which is paid for that freedom. (Swinburne 1998, 17)

Swinburne argues along this line because he works with the assumption that God possesses the omni-properties and can adequately compensate the sufferer in this life or in the hereafter. The consolation God lacks this capacity. His goodness and limited powers only allow him to empathise with creatures and to ameliorate their suffering where he is able to do so (being morally responsible). The freedom factor cannot be invoked because in a universe of yearning, diverse causes condition conduct, although creatures are ultimately responsible for their actions given the fact that they can distinguish between right and wrong. Recall that a universe animated by *mood* is not rigidly determined. From the foregoing, the consolationist God does not have the right to create a world marred by evil.

> *If the consolationist account of a passible, empathetic God is true, how can humans know that God is ameliorating the suffering in the world?*

Now, a God of consolation is one who can offer succour to creatures that suffer in varying degrees in an imperfect world that exhibits moral and physical evil. Lacking the omni-properties, the consolation God cannot do all (logically possible) things. But as a powerful, knowledgeable, and good creator, he can ameliorate at least some of the suffering in the world. The empirically minded objector may wonder how humans can know or discern that the consolation God indeed ameliorates the suffering in the world. The question now is not whether he exists, since we are working with the assumption that he exists. As I have observed elsewhere (Agada 2023a), instead of appealing to miraculous interventions that the sceptic will always doubt, one can invoke the factor of belief which maintains logical coherence within the consolationist system. God ameliorates the suffering in the world using human moral agency. Being of a much more majestic order than humans, he cannot materialise and mingle with humans while overseeing palliative processes aimed at reducing the suffering in the world. At the point of creation, the consolation God manipulated *mood* in such a way that the idea of a morality-loving God is implanted in the consciousness of the human being, such that when this being thinks about goodness it also contemplates the idea of a good creator of the world who shares in human suffering. The idea of a good creator is such that it invites humans to try as much as possible to emulate the consolation God and strive towards perfection, impossible as this goal may be. Morality, when understood in terms of consolation, invites thinking and sentient beings to expand the sphere of goodness. Since God is the highest consolation, he motivates human moral behaviour. Those who believe in him consciously strive to emulate him, thereby reducing the suffering in the world. Those who do not believe in him may unwittingly emulate him, since he has planted the seed of the active striving after goodness in human consciousness, thereby reducing the evil in the world.

3.6 Conclusion

This section brings this Element to an end. In this section, I showed how consolationist metaphysics makes a contribution to contemporary African philosophy of religion. After reviewing the literature in the first two sections of this Element, I focused effort on delineating the powers of the consolation God in this section. Specifically, I showed in Section 1 that there are two broad conceptions of God in ATR and introduced the reader to the limitation thesis of African limited God proponents. The two conceptions are traditional African theism and the African limited God view. I focused effort on the exposition and analysis of the limited God stances of philosophers in the vitalist and non-vitalist traditions like Wiredu, Bewaji, the Chimakonams, Molefe, Attoe, and Ofuasia. In Section 2, I explored the implication of the various views held by African limited God philosophers for the problem of evil and concluded that the logical and evidential problem of evil does not arise in African philosophy of religion. Nevertheless, I pointed out that even a limited God has moral responsibility for the evil in the world in his capacity as the creator.

The question of how the limited God is morally responsible for the evil in the world is the dominant question of Section 3. I engaged the question from the perspective of the philosophy of consolationism that asserts that imperfection characterises a universe animated by *mood*. Making a unique contribution to the literature, I demonstrated in Section 3 that the *mood*-constituted God is properly a consolation God who can be deemed to be working towards the amelioration of the suffering in the world. I explored the question of the consolation God's moral responsibility and denied that he has a right to create a world marred by evil. I argued that this God is a possible being who is obliged to ameliorate the suffering of his creatures. Future writings on the nature and capacities of the consolation God will more broadly focus on a comparison of the consolation God with the Christian God and the God of Hindu traditions in what will count as a contribution to global philosophy of religion just like the current Element.

References

Abimbola, Kola. 2006. *Yoruba culture: A philosophical account*. Birmingham: Iroko Academic.

Abraham, W. Emmanuel. 2010. Crisis in African culture. In *Person and community: Ghanaian philosophical studies I*, edited by Kwasi Wiredu and Kwame Gyekye, 13–35. Washington, DC: Council for Research in Values and Philosophy.

Agada, Ada. 2015. *Existence and consolation: Reinventing ontology, gnosis, and values in African philosophy*. St. Paul, MN: Paragon House.

Agada, Ada. 2019. Rethinking the metaphysical questions of mind, matter, freedom, determinism, purpose, and the mind–body problem within the panpsychist framework of consolationism. *South African Journal of Philosophy* 38(1): 1–16. https://doi.org/10.1080/02580136.2018.1560589.

Agada, Ada. 2020a. Grounding the consolationist concept of mood in the African vital force theory. *Philosophia Africana* 19(2): 101–121. http://doi.org/10.5325/philafri.19.2.0101.

Agada, Ada. 2020b. Complementarism and consolationism: Mapping out a 21st century African philosophical trajectory. *Synthesis Philosophica* 69(1) (2020): 135–153. https://doi.org/10.21464/sp35108.

Agada, Ada. 2022a. Bewaji and Fayemi on God, omnipotence, and evil. *Filosofia Theoretica: Journal of African Philosophy, Culture, and Religions* 11(1): 41–56. https://doi.org/10.4314/ft.v11i1.4.

Agada, Ada. 2022b. *Consolationism and comparative African philosophy: Beyond universalism and particularism*. London: Routledge.

Agada, Ada. 2023a. Rethinking the concept of God and the problem of evil from the perspective of African thought. *Religious Studies* 59: 294–310. https://doi.org/10.1017/S0034412522000294.

Agada, Ada. 2023b. Between sense-phenomenalism, equi-phenomenalism, quasi-physicalism, and panpsychism. In *Conversations on African philosophy of mind, consciousness, and artificial intelligence*, edited by Aribiah D. Attoe, Samuel T. Segun, Victor Nweke, Umezurike J. Ezugwu, and Jonathan O. Chimakonam, 37–48. Cham: Springer.

Agada, Ada. 2023c. God's existence and the problem of evil in African philosophy of religion. In *Handbook of African philosophy*, edited by Elvis Imafidon, Mpho Tshivase, and Björn Freter, 555–574. Cham: Springer.

Agada, Ada, and Uti Ojah Egbai. 2018. Language, thought and interpersonal communication: A cross-cultural conversation on the question of individuality and community. *Filosofia Theoretica: Journal of African Philosophy, Culture and Religions* 7(2): 141–162. https://doi.org/10.4314/ft.v7i2.9.

Aja, Egbeke. 1996. The supreme God in an African (Igbo) religious thought. *Philosophy in the Contemporary World* 3(4): 1–7. https://doi.org/10.5840/pcw19963415.

Alston, William P. 1991. The inductive argument from evil and the human cognitive condition. *Philosophical Perspectives* 5: 29–67.

Asouzu, Innocent I. 2007. *Ibuaru̱: The heavy burden of philosophy beyond African philosophy.* Zurich: LIT Verlag GmbH & Company.

Attoe, A. David 2022a. *Towards a new kind of African metaphysics: The idea of predeterministic historicity.* Cham: Palgrave Macmillan.

Attoe, A. David. 2022b. Redefining the problem of evil in the context of a predeterministic world: New conversations with the traditional African worldview. *Filosofia Theoretica: Journal of African Philosophy, Culture, and Religions* 11(1): 9–26. https://doi.org/10.4314/ft.v11i1.2.

Attoe, A. David. 2022c. Cosmic purpose: An African perspective. *Filosofia Theoretica: Journal of African Philosophy, Culture, and Religions* 11(4): 87–102.

Attoe, A. David. 2023. Death and meaning(lessness): Re-examining the African view. *Religious Studies* 59: 311–325. https://doi.org/10.1017/S0034412522000415.

Awolalu, Joseph Omosade, and P. Adelumo Dopamu. 1979. *West African traditional religion.* Ibadan: Onibonoje Press.

Balogun, Oladele A. 2009. The nature of evil and human wickedness in traditional African thought: Further reflections on the philosophical problem of evil. *Lumina* 20(2): 1–20.

Behrens, Kevin. 2010. Exploring African holism with respect to the environment. *Environmental Values* 19(4): 465–484.

Benatar, David. 2006. *Better never to have been.* New York: Oxford University Press.

Bergmann, Michael. 2009. Sceptical theism and the problem of evil. In *Oxford handbook of philosophical theology,* edited by Thomas Flint and Michael Rea, 375–399. Oxford: Oxford University Press.

Bewaji, John Ayotunde I. 1998. Olodumare: God in Yoruba belief and the theistic problem of evil. *African Studies Quarterly* 2(1): 1–17. www.africa.ufl.edu/asq/v2/v2i1a1.pdf.

Bodunrin, Peter. 1981. The question of African philosophy. *Philosophy* 56 (216): 161–179.

Bortolotti, Lisa, and Yujin Nagasawa. 2009. Immortality without boredom. *Ratio* 22(3): 261–277.

Bujo, Bénézet. 2001. *Foundations of an African ethic*. Translated by B. Mcneil. New York: Crossroad.

Burley, Mikel. 2020. African religions, mythic narratives, and conceptual enrichment in the philosophy of religion. *Religious Studies* 1–17. Advance online version. https://doi.org/10.1017/S0034412520000086.

Chimakonam, Amara E. 2022. Why the problem of evil might not be a problem after all in African philosophy of religion. *Filosofia Theoretica: Journal of African Philosophy, Culture, and Religions* 11(1): 27–40. https://doi.org/10.4314/ft.v11i1.3.

Chimakonam, Jonathan O., and Amara E. Chimakonam. 2023. Examining the logical argument of the problem of evil from an African perspective. *Religious Studies* 59: 326–339. https://doi.org/10.1017/S0034412522000300.

Chow, Dawn Eschenauer. 2018. The passibility of God: A plea for analogy. *Faith and Philosophy* 35(4): 389–407.

Chuwa, L. T. 2014. *African indigenous ethics in global bioethics: Interpreting Ubuntu*. New York: Springer.

Cordeiro-Rodrigues, Luis. 2021. Mutability and relationality: Towards an African four- dimensionalist pan-psychism. *Religions* 12: 1094. Advance online version. https://doi.org/10.3390/rel12121094.

Cordeiro-Rodrigues. Luis. 2023. Engaging and developing Ada Agada's philosophy: Moral responsibility, creation, and the problem of evil. *Religious Studies* 1–10. Advance online version. https://10.1017/S0034412523000513.

Cordeiro-Rodrigues, Luis, and Ada Agada. 2022. African philosophy of religion: Concepts of God, ancestors, and the problem of evil. *Philosophy Compass* 17(8):1–11. https://doi.org/10.1111/phc3.12864.

Cordeiro-Rodrigues, Luis, and Jonathan O. Chimakonam. 2022. The logical problem of evil and African war ethics. *Journal of Military Ethics*. 1–14. Advance online version. https://doi.org/10.1080/15027570.2022.2158949.

Cordeiro-Rodrigues, Luis, and Jonathan O. Chimakonam. 2023. The problem of evil from a decolonial viewpoint. *Philosophia: International Journal of Philosophy* 24(1): 51–72.

Danquah, Joseph Boakye. 1944. *The Akan doctrine of God*. London: Lutterworth.

Diop, Cheikh Anta. 1974. *The African origin of civilization: Myth or reality*. New York: Lawrence Hill Books.

Dukor, Maduabuchi. 1990. God and godlings in African ontology. *Indian Philosophical Quarterly*, 17(1), 75–89.

Dzobo, Noah K. 2010. Values in a changing society: Man, ancestors, and God. In *Person and community: Ghanaian philosophical Studies I*, edited by Kwasi Wiredu and Kwame Gyekye, 223–240. Washington, DC: Council for Research in Values and Philosophy.

Ebo, Socrates. 2022. Random thoughts on the concept of mind in a material cosmos. *Global Journal of Arts, Humanities, and Social Sciences* 10(5): 15–24.

Ehrlich, Paul. 1968. *The population bomb*. New York: Ballantine Books.

Etieyibo, Edwin. 2017. Anthropocentrism, African metaphysical worldview, and animal practice: A reply to Kai Horsthemke. *Journal of Animal Ethics* 7(2): 145–162.

Eze, Michael O. 2008. What is African communitarianism? Against consensus as a regulative ideal. *South African Journal of Philosophy* 27(4): 386–399.

Ezekwugo, C. U. M. 1987. Chi: *The true God in Igbo religion*. Muvattupuzha : Mar Matthew Press.

Famakinwa, J. O. 2010. How moderate is Kwame Gyekye's moderate communitarianism? *Thought and Practice* 2: 65–77.

Fayemi, Ademola K. 2012. Philosophical problem of evil: Response to E. O. Oduwole. *Philosophia: International Journal of Philosophy* 41(1): 1–15.

Gbadegesin, Segun. 1991. *African philosophy: Traditional Yoruba philosophy and contemporary African realities*. New York: Peter Lang.

Gwara, Joyline, and L. Uchenna Ogbonnaya. 2022. Rethinking God's omnibenevolence and omnipotence in the light of the COVID-19 pandemic: An African perspective. *Filosofia Theoretica: Journal of African Philosophy, Culture, and Religions* 11(4): 31–52. https://dx.doi.org/10.4314/ft.v11i4.3s.

Gyekye, Kwame. 1995. *An essay on African philosophical thought: The Akan conceptual scheme*. Rev. ed. Philadelphia, PA: Temple University Press.

Hallen, Barry. 2002. *A short history of African philosophy*. Bloomington: Indiana University Press.

Hartshorne, Charles. 1948. *The divine relativity: A social conception of God*. New Haven, CT: Yale University Press.

Hegel, Georg Wilhelm Friedrich. [1824] 2001. *The philosophy of history*. Translated by J. Sibree. Kitchener: Batoche Books.

Hick, John. 1966. *Evil and the God of love*. New York: Harper and Row.

Horsthemke, Kai. 2017. Animals and African ethics. *Journal of Animal Ethics* 7(2): 119–144.

Hume, David. [1777] 1987. Of national characters. In *Essays: Moral, political, and literary*, edited by Eugene F. Miller, 197–225. Indianapolis, IN: Liberty Fund.

Hume, David. [1779] 2007. *Dialogue concerning natural religion and other writings*, edited by Dorothy Coleman. Cambridge: Cambridge University Press.

Idowu, E. Bolaji. 1962. Olodumare: *God in Yoruba belief*. London: Longmans.

Idowu, E. Bolaji. 1973. *African traditional religion: A definition*. London: SCM Press.

Ikenga-Metuh, E. 1981. *God and man in African religion*. London: Geoffrey Chapman.

Ikuenobe, Polycarp A. 2014. Traditional African environmental ethics and colonial legacy. *International Journal of Philosophy and Theology* 2(4): 1–21.

Kane, Stanley G. 1975. The failure of soul-making theodicy. *International Journal for Philosophy of Religion*. 6(1): 1–22.

Kaphagawani, Didier N. 2004. African conceptions of a person: A critical survey. In *A Companion to African Philosophy*, edited by Kwasi Wiredu, 332–342. Oxford: Blackwell.

Kopel, Jonathan, Franklyn C. Babb, William Hasker, Mark Webb, Carmine C. Gorga, K. J. Oommen, Gregory L. Brower, and Andrew Coleman. 2022. Suffering and divine impassibility. *Baylor University Medical Center Proceedings* 35(1): 139–141. https://doi.org/10.1080/08998280.2021.1981674.

Lougheed, Kirk, Motsamai Molefe, and Thaddeus Metz. 2024. *African philosophy of religion and Western monotheism*. Cambridge: Cambridge University Press.

Macquarrie, John. 1978. *The humility of God*. Philadelphia, PA: Westminster Press.

Magesa, Laurenti. 1997. *African religion: The moral tradition of abundant life*. Maryknoll, NY: Orbis Books.

Majeed, Hasskei M. 2018. Moderate communitarianism is different: A response to J. O. Famakinwa and B. Matolino. *Journal of Philosophy and Culture* 6(1): 3–15.

Makinde, Moses A. 2007. *African philosophy: The demise of a controversy*. Ile-Ife: Obafemi Awolowo University Press.

Mangena, Fainos. 2014. Ethno-philosophy is rational: A reply to two famous critics. *Thought and Practice* 6(2): 23–38. https://doi.org/10.4314/tp.v6i2.3.

Masolo, Dismas A. 1994. *African philosophy in search of identity*. Bloomington: Indiana University Press.

Matolino, Bernard. 2015. Universalism and African philosophy. *South African Journal of Philosophy* 34(4): 433–440.

Mbiti, John S. 1969. *African religions and philosophy*. London: Heinemann.

Mbiti, John S. 1975. *Introduction to African religion*. London: Heinemann.

Menkiti, Ifeanyi. 1984. Person and community in African traditional thought. In *African philosophy: An introduction*. 3rd ed., edited by Richard A. Wright, 171–181. Lanham, MD: University Press of America.

Menkiti, Ifeanyi. 2004. On the normative conception of a person. In *A Companion to African Philosophy*, edited by Kwasi Wiredu, 324–331. Oxford: Blackwell.

Metz, Thaddeus. 2012a. *Meaning in life: An analytic study*. Oxford: Oxford University Press.

Metz, Thaddeus. 2012b. Contemporary anti-natalism, featuring Benatar's *Better never to have been. South African Journal of Philosophy* 31(1): 1–9.

Molefe, Motsamai. 2018. African metaphysics and religious ethics. *Filosofia Theoretica: Journal of African Philosophy, Culture, and Religions* 7(3): 19–37. https://doi.org/10.4314/ft.v7i3.3.

Molefe, Motsamai, and Mutshidzi Maraganedzha. 2023. African traditional religion and moral philosophy. *Religious Studies* 59: 355–370. https://doi .org/10.1017/S0034412522000543.

Moltmann, Jürgen. 1993. *The crucified God: The cross of Christ as the foundation and criticism of Christian theology.* Translated by R. A. Wilson and John Bowden. Minneapolis, MN: Fortress Books.

Momoh, Campbell S. 1985. African philosophy . . . Does it exist? *Diogenes* 130: 73–104.

More, Mabogo P. 1996. African philosophy revisited. *Alternation* 3(1): 109–129.

Mosima, Pius. 2022. African approaches to God, death, and the problem of evil: Some anthropological lessons towards an intercultural philosophy of religion. *Filosofia Theoretica: Journal of African Philosophy, Culture, and Religions* 11(4): 151–168. https://dx.doi.org/10.4314/ft.v11i4.10s.

Mudimbe, Valentin-Yves. 1988. *The invention of Africa: Gnosis, philosophy and the order of knowledge.* Bloomington: Indiana University Press.

Njoku, Francis O. C. 2002. *Essays in African philosophy, thought and theology.* Owerri: Claretian Institute of Philosophy.

Nkemnkia, Martin. 1999. *African vitalogy: A step forward in African thinking.* Nairobi: Paulines Publications Africa.

Nkondo, Gessler M. 2007. Ubuntu as a public policy in South Africa: A conceptual framework. *International Journal of African Renaissance Studies* 2: 88–100.

Nwoga, Donatus I. 1984. *The supreme God as a stranger in Igboland.* Imo: Hawk Press.

Nze, Chukwuemeka. 1981. Pragmatism and traditionalism in the conception of God in Africa. *Uche* 5(1): 15–31.

Oduwole, Ebunoluwa O. 2007. The dialectics of *ire* (goodness) and *ibi* (evilness): An African understanding of the philosophical problem of evil. *Philosophia: International Journal of Philosophy* 36(1): 1–13.

Ofuasia, Emmanuel. 2022a. Who/what neglected monotheism? A panentheistic rejoinder to Thaddeus Metz and Motsamai Molefe on African Traditional Religion. *Philosophia Africana* 21(2): 78–99. https://doi.org/10.5325/ philafri.21.2.0078.

Ofuasia, Emmanuel. 2022b. An argument for the non-existence of the devil in African traditional religions. *Filosofia Theoretica: Journal of African*

Philosophy, Culture, and Religions 11(1): 57–76. https://doi.org/10.4314/ft.11i1.5.

Ofuasia, Emmanuel. 2022c. The challenge of the 'end of metaphysics' for ethnophilosophy: A discourse on the process implication of the metaphysics of terror. In *Ethnophilosophy and the search for the wellspring of African philosophy*, edited by Ada Agada, 271–285. Cham: Springer. https://doi.org/10.1007/978-3-030-78897-1.

Oguejiofor, J. Obi. 2009. Negritude as hermeneutics: A reinterpretation of Léopold Sédar Senghor's philosophy. *American Catholic Philosophical Quarterly* 83(1): 79–94.

Ojimba, Anthony C., and Victor I. Chidubem. 2022. The concept of God in Igbo traditional religious thought. *Filosofia Theoretica: Journal of African Philosophy, Culture, and Religions* 11(4): 103–120. https://dx.doi.org/10.4314/ft.v11i4.7s.

Okere, Theophilus. 1983. *African philosophy: A historico-hermeneutical investigation of the conditions of its possibilities*. Lanham, MD: University Press of America.

Oladipo, Olusegun. 2004. Religion in African culture: Some conceptual issues. In *A companion to African philosophy*, edited by Kwasi Wiredu, 355–363. Oxford: Blackwell.

Onyewuenyi, Innocent C. 1993. *The African origin of Greek philosophy*. Nsukka: University of Nigeria Press.

Otte, Richard. 2009. Transworld depravity and unobtainable worlds. *Philosophy and Phenomenological Research* 78(1): 165–177.

Outlaw, Lucius T. 2004. Africana philosophy: Origin and prospects. In *A companion to African philosophy*, edited by Kwasi Wiredu. 90–98. Oxford: Blackwell.

Oyowe, A. Oritsegbubemi, and Olga Yurkivska. 2014. Can a communitarian concept of African personhood be both relational and gender-neutral? *South African Journal of Philosophy* 33: 85–99.

Parker, Gordon. 2013. A case for reprising and redefining melancholia. *Canadian Journal of Psychiatry* 58: 183–189. https://doi.org/10.1177/070674371305800402.

Parrinder, Edward Geoffrey. 1954. *African Traditional Religion*. London: Hutchinson.

p'Bitek, Okot. 1971. *African religions in Western scholarship*. Nairobi: Kenya Literature Bureau.

p'Bitek, Okot. 2011. *Decolonizing African religions: A short history of African religions in Western scholarship*. New York: Diasporic Africa Press.

Pinnock, C. H., R. Rice, J. Sanders, W. Hasker, and D. Basinger. 1994. *The openness of God: A biblical challenge to the traditional understanding of God*. Downers Grove, IL: InterVarsity Press.

Plantinga, Alvin. 1965. The free will defense. In *Philosophy in America*, edited by Max Black, 204–220. London: Allen and Unwin.

Plantinga, Alvin. 1977. *God, freedom, and evil*. Grand Rapids, MI: William B. Eerdmans.

Ramose, Mogobe B. 1991. Hegel and universalism: An African perspective. *Dialogue and Humanism* 1(1): 75–87.

Rowe, William. 1979. The problem of evil and some varieties of atheism. *American Philosophical Quarterly* 16: 335–341.

Rudy-Hiller, Fernando. 2022. The epistemic condition for moral responsibility. In *Stanford Encyclopedia of Philosophy*, edited by E. N. Zalta and U. Nodelman. https://plato.stanford.edu/archives/win2022/entries/moral-responsibility-epistemic.

Schopenhauer, Arthur. 2000. *Parerga and paralipomena, vol. 1*. Translated by E. F. J. Payne. Oxford: Oxford University Press.

Scrutton, Anastasia. 2013. Divine passibility: God and emotions. *Philosophy Compass* 8(9): 866–874.

Senghor, Léopold Sédar. 1964. *On African socialism*. Translated by Mercer Cook. London: Pall Mall.

Shaw, Rosalind. 1990. The invention of 'African Traditional Religion'. *Religion* 20: 339–353.

Singh, Asheel. 2012. Furthering the case for anti-natalism: Seana Shiffrin and the limits of permissible harm. *South African Journal of Philosophy* 31(1): 104–116.

Sodipo, John O. 1975. Philosophy in Africa today. *Thought and Practice* 2(2): 115–123.

Sogolo, Godwin S. 1993. *Foundations of African philosophy: A definitive analysis of conceptual issues in African thought*. Ibadan: Ibadan University Press.

Sterba, James P. 2019 *Is a good God logically possible?* Cham: Palgrave Macmillan.

Strawson, Peter F. 1962. Freedom and resentment. *Proceedings of the British Academy* 48: 1–25.

Stump, Eleonore. 1985. The problem of evil. *Faith and Philosophy* 2(4): 392–423.

Swinburne, Richard. 1998. *Providence and the problem of evil*. Oxford: Clarendon.

Taiwo, Olufemi. 1998. Exorcizing Hegel's ghost: Africa's challenge to philosophy. *African Studies Quarterly* 1(4): 1–16. www.africa.ufl.edu/asq/v1/4/2.pdf.

Taringa, Nisbert. 2006. How environmental is African traditional religion? *Exchange* 35(2): 191–214.

Teffo, Joe. 2004. Democracy, kingship, and consensus: A South African perspective. In *A companion to African philosophy*, edited by Kwasi Wiredu, 443–449. Oxford: Blackwell.

Tempels, Placide. 1959. *Bantu philosophy*. Translated by C. King. Paris: Présence Africaine.

Tutu, Desmond. 1999. *No future without forgiveness*. New York: Random House

Ukpong, Justin S. 1983. The problem of God and sacrifice in African Traditional Religion. *Journal of Religion in Africa* 14(3): 187–203.

Whitehead, Alfred North. 1978. *Process and reality: An essay in cosmology*. New York: Free Press.

Williams, Bernard. 1973. The Makropulos case: Reflections on the tedium of immortality. In *Problems of the self*, edited by Bernard Williams, 82–100. Cambridge: Cambridge University Press.

Wiredu, Kwasi. 1992. African philosophical tradition: A case study of the Akan. *The Philosophical Forum* 24(1–3): 35–62.

Wiredu, Kwasi. 1996. *Cultural universals and particulars: An African perspective*. Indianapolis: Indiana University Press.

Wiredu, Kwasi. 1998. Toward decolonizing African philosophy and religion. *African Studies Quarterly* 1(4): 17–46. http://africa.ufl.edu/asq/v1/4/3.pdf.

Wiredu, Kwasi. 2010. The moral foundations of an African culture. In *Person and community: Ghanaian philosophical studies I*, edited by Kwasi Wiredu and Kwame Gyekye, 193–206. Washington, DC: Council for Research in Values and Philosophy.

Wiredu, Kwasi. 2013. African religions. In *The Routledge companion to philosophy of religion*, edited by C. Meister and P. Copan, 29–38. London: Routledge.

Wykstra, Stephen J. 1984. The human obstacle to evidential arguments from suffering: On avoiding the evils of 'appearance'. *International Journal for Philosophy of Religion* 16: 73–93.

Acknowledgements

I hasten to express my profound gratitude to the Vice Chancellor of Federal University Otuoke, Prof. Teddy Charles Adias, for providing me a platform on which I could thrive and for making Otuoke my intellectual home.

My heartfelt gratitude goes to my indefatigable brother, Dr Akogwu Agada, for his unshakable faith in the value of my scholarly endeavour.

I thank my supportive Head of Department, Dr Socrates Ebo. I am grateful to my respected colleagues at the Department of Philosophy, Rev. Fr (Dr) Bruno Yammeluan Ikuli, Dr Thaddeus Oparah, and Mr Azibaolanami Iworiso, for their intellectual friendship.

I am grateful to the urbane Dean, Faculty of Humanities, Federal University Otuoke, Prof. Akachi Odoemene, and to my respected friend Prof. Osakue S. Omoera, for making me feel welcome at Federal University Otuoke.

Cambridge Elements $\equiv$

Global Philosophy of Religion

Yujin Nagasawa

University of Oklahoma

Yujin Nagasawa is Kingfisher College Chair of the Philosophy of Religion and Ethics and Professor of Philosophy at the University of Oklahoma. He is the author of *The Problem of Evil for Atheists* (2024), *Maximal God: A New Defence of Perfect Being Theism* (2018), *Miracles: A Very Short Introduction* (2018), *The Existence of God: A Philosophical Introduction* (2011), and *God and Phenomenal Consciousness* (2008), along with numerous articles. He is the editor-in-chief of *Religious Studies* and served as the president of the British Society for the Philosophy of Religion from 2017 to 2019.

About the Series

This Cambridge Elements series provides concise and structured overviews of a wide range of religious beliefs and practices, with an emphasis on global, multi-faith viewpoints. Leading scholars from diverse cultural backgrounds and geographical regions explore topics and issues that have been overlooked by Western philosophy of religion.

Cambridge Elements ⁼

Global Philosophy of Religion

Elements in the Series

Afro-Brazilian Religions
José Eduardo Porcher

The African Mood *Perspective on God and the Problem of Evil*
Ada Agada

A full series listing is available at: www.cambridge.org/EGPR